W9-BRO-825

just Jesus

MARK WITAS

YOUNG ADULT DEVOTIONAL

REVIEW AND HERALD® PUBLISHING ASSOCIATION
Since 1861 | www.reviewandherald.com

Copyright © 2014 by Review and Herald® Publishing Association

Published by Review and Herald® Publishing Association, Hagerstown, MD 21741-1119

All rights reserved. No portion of this book may be reproduced, stored in a retrieval system, or transmitted in any form or by any means (electronic, mechanical, photocopy, recording, scanning, or other), except for brief quotations in critical reviews or articles, without the prior written permission of the publisher.

Review and Herald® titles may be purchased in bulk for educational, business, fund-raising, or sales promotional use. For information, e-mail SpecialMarkets@reviewandherald.com

Unless otherwise noted, Bible texts in this book are from the *Holy Bible, New International Version.* Copyright © 1973, 1978, 1984, 2011 by Biblica, Inc. Used by permission. All rights reserved worldwide.

Texts credited to KJV are from the King James Version.

Scripture quotations marked NASB are from the *New American Standard Bible,* copyright © 1960, 1962, 1963, 1968, 1971, 1972, 1973, 1975, 1977, 1995 by The Lockman Foundation. Used by permission.

Texts credited to NKJV are from the New King James Version. Copyright © 1970, 1980, 1982 by Thomas Nelson, Inc. Used by permission. All rights reserved.

Scripture quotations marked NLT are taken from the *Holy Bible*, New Living Translation, copyright © 1996, 2004, 2007 by Tyndale House Foundation. Used by permission of Tyndale House Publishers, Inc., Carol Stream, Illinois 60188. All rights reserved.

This book was
Edited by Gerald Wheeler
Copyedited by Megan Mason
Design by Ron J. Pride / Review and Herald® Design Center

PRINTED IN U.S.A.
18 17 16 15 14 5 4 3 2 1

Library of Congress Cataloging-in-Publication Data
Witas, Mark, 1962- .
Just Jesus / Mark Witas.
pages cm
ISBN 978-0-8280-2797-7
1. Jesus Christ. 2. Seventh-day Adventists—Doctrines. I. Title.
BT203.W57 2014
232—dc23
2014009988

ISBN 978-0-8280-2797-7

contents

about the author

For the past 20 years Mark Witas has been following Jesus as a pastor, a teacher, a chaplain, and a featured speaker at special events around the world. He has a special place in his heart for rhubarb pie, and is currently the lead pastor at the Pacific Union College church in Angwin, California.

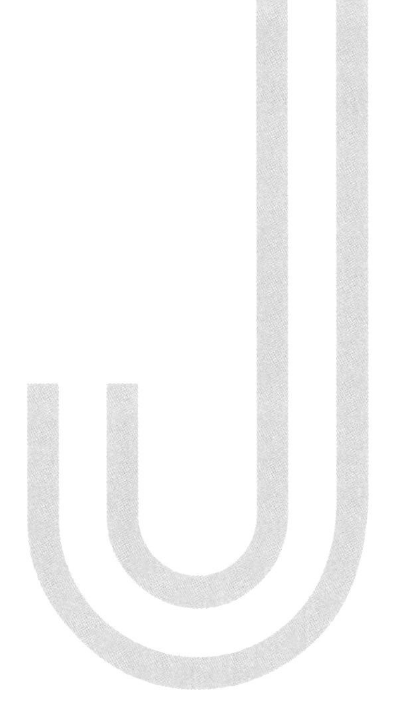

For I decided that . . .

I would forget **everything**

except Jesus Christ,

the one who was crucified.

—1 Cor. 2:2, NLT

CHAPTER 1

Jesus and Doctrine

Doctrine. It's such a cold word—almost like a swearword. "Oh, yeah! Well, you're full of doctrine!" Or perhaps it sounds like a place where good ideas go to die. Doctrine.

I can't tell you how many times I've had church members ask me, "Why do we have 28 fundamental beliefs? Are there exactly 28 things we are supposed to believe in? What if I'm only invested in 25 of them—do I still belong?" Twenty-five out of 28 is 89 percent. That's a strong B+! Can I be a good Adventist with a B+? Does 89 percent of Adventist doctrine get you into heaven?

It's been my experience that many in the Seventh-day Adventist Church view our doctrine as a collection of beliefs that define us and separate us from Babylon. But I would like to suggest that that is a gross misunderstanding of what doctrine is for. Instead, rather than using our doctrine to define us as a church, our church's doctrine ought to be a biblical expression of the God we believe in. I think this particular view is more relevant than ever to the Seventh-day Adventist Church and its members today. Let me explain by retelling a story you are well familiar with. Adventists call it the great controversy.

A long, long time ago, far, far away, the Bible says that a war raged in heaven. Scripture says that the dragon that initiated the conflict was dragging God's name through the mud—trying to elevate himself above the Deity that created him. It earned Satan and his angels a ticket out of heaven.

And then one day, as Eve was walking through the garden, the snake in the tree said, "Did God really tell you not to eat from this tree?" In other words: Who is God to tell you what to do? Who made Him your boss? Eve begins to question God's authority.

The dragon continued his onslaught. "God said you would die if you eat the fruit? You will not surely die." He put in her head the idea that maybe God isn't trustworthy. Perhaps, even, He was a liar.

And then the final blow. "If you eat the fruit, you will be just like God, knowing good from evil." Eve's mind was reeling now. *Is God holding out on me? Is He not giving me what I should rightfully have?*

She used to think that the tree was bad and that God was good. Now she saw the tree as good and God as bad.

In deceiving Adam and Eve, the dragon warped the human idea about God. Revelation 12:9 says: "And the great dragon was thrown down, the serpent of old who is called the devil and Satan, who deceives the whole world; he was thrown down to the earth, and his angels were thrown down with him" (NASB).

Scripture tells us that the dragon intends to deceive the whole world about who God is. His plan was successful in the garden, and he is still using it.

But God also had a plan. He established a people to represent Him on earth. The seed of Abraham were to learn of Him, know Him, and shine as a light to the whole world—to show and tell the world the truth about a loving God. Israel was to reveal the Father to the world.

Hosea 11:1 refers to Israel as the "son" of God. As they developed their worship practices and their doctrine, they fell into the horrible trap of having their doctrine define and separate them as a people instead of letting it point to and speak of a God of grace that wants to bless, redeem, and save.

Anytime a group of people use doctrine to define themselves rather than establishing doctrine to explain and clarify God, they will yield to the very real temptation of considering themselves apart from and better than the rest of the world. And this will ultimately do damage to God's character, no matter what truth they may possess.

Israel did wound God's character. But He still had a plan.

God wanted to be reconciled to His people. He desired that they know who He truly is. So the mystery of God was revealed when He put on flesh and became a human being. Jesus received the same task as Israel—to clarify the Father. And He was also called God's Son.

John 1:18 tells us that "no one has seen God at any time; the only begotten God who is in the bosom of the Father, He has explained Him" (NASB).

Even though they had all of the books of the Old Testament, God's people still had a very warped idea of who He was. Jesus came to explain the Father in a way that Old Testament scripture evidently could not do.

Jesus declared, "If you have seen Me, you've seen the Father" (see John 15:9). He became the doctrine of God in the flesh. Jesus is the doctrine of God.

More than anything or anyone else in the history of the world, Jesus is the revelation of the true character of God. And notice the difference between His representations of the Father and how the doctrine of the "church" in Jesus' day revealed Him:

- Jesus took the nature of a servant. The religious leaders lorded over their people and looked down on the world.
- Jesus mixed with sinners. God's people shunned them.
- Jesus included and redeemed. The church of the time separated itself and condemned . . . in the name of God.

Instead of showing the world the love of the Father, the doctrine of Israel ended up alienating and separating. Jesus had to come to become doctrine in flesh.

So when He went back to heaven to sit at the right hand side of the Father, He handed the responsibility of revealing the Father to us, His New Testament church. He left us, the sons and daughters of God, in charge of revealing the Father to a dying world.

History tells us that it wasn't long before the church started going down the same road as the nation of Israel had. All too quickly it warped and perverted God's character. Becoming rich and self-absorbed, it began to use force instead of love. It started to teach things about God that created a gulf between the Father and His people.

Instead of focusing on the life and death and resurrection of Jesus, the church again began to create doctrine to define and set itself apart. Even worse, it employed doctrine to impose its will and to try to control people spiritually. And it used fear as a tactic to manipulate and coerce.

And so it started to teach such things as "God loves you. But if you don't love Him back, He'll get angry and throw you into an ever-burning inferno, making sure that you are there for all eternity." With this concept the church turned God into a volatile psychopath.

It began to claim that God is unapproachable—that instead of going to Him with your burdens, you have to visit a priest. Now God is aloof.

Theologians declared that babies were born lost and that if you didn't baptize them shortly after birth and they died, they'd suffer an eternity in hell. God can't save babies.

Eventually they offered forgiveness for money—the ability to sin and not be held accountable. Just pay the right price. The rich have better access to heaven.

Finally they elevated human teachings and traditions above the will of God as written in the Holy Scriptures and revealed in the life of Christ.

And if you didn't agree with the church's doctrine? Economic sanctions, imprisonment, or death by fire while tied to a stake.

Jesus saw what His church would one day become. In John 16:2 He warned the disciples, "They will put you out of the synagogue; in fact, the time is coming when anyone who kills you will think they are offering a service to God."

Is it possible to be so blinded by your own doctrine that you would actually take human life in God's name and think you are doing Him a service?

The book of Revelation prophetically describes the church of the Middle Ages as something that looks like the Lamb, but speaks like a dragon.

The church failed miserably at letting Jesus' life, death, and resurrection define its doctrine. Instead, it used doctrine as a way to coerce people into acting the way they wanted.

The great danger of doctrine is that we can use it to manipulate people to join a church, to stay in a church, to contribute to a church, or to define a church. Doctrine can cause a church to look like the Lamb, but speak and act like the dragon.

I believe strongly that this is where the prophetic calling of the Seventh-day Adventist Church comes into play. The primary purpose of our movement is to tell the world the truth about God—to dispel the false picture of Him that the church has saturated the world with for centuries.

The books of Daniel and Revelation prophesy about the rise of a people that would receive the task of cleaning up the lies about God that the dragon and church have littered the world with.

Seventh-day Adventism had an awkward beginning, didn't it? We developed out of a movement that was dead wrong about the date of Jesus' return. But out of that great disappointment grew a people voraciously devoted to studying the Bible and banking on being with Jesus as soon as He would allow. They longed to be with Him.

As they developed into an actual movement—into a church—they discovered things in the Bible that nobody else was teaching about God. Those new discoveries were exciting!

It turned out that God wasn't the aloof tyrant that the church had painted Him to be, running hot and cold in His feelings toward us. In fact, God was a lot more like Jesus than the leaders of the church had ever taught Him to be.

So, through much study, our evolving church began to establish doctrine. And through the years this has been both a good thing and a bad thing.

It was a good thing in that our doctrine paints a beautiful picture of God, who, as it turns out, is just like Jesus. But we have not always used or taught doctrine well.

Someone very close to me is an atheist. She grew up in the Seventh-day Adventist Church at a time when I believe people employed doctrine to define and separate the church instead of revealing the grace of God through Jesus Christ.

During her childhood and youth, teachers explained the sanctuary doctrine this way: Starting in 1844, God opened up some books. In one of those books is your name. When He gets to your name, He is going to look at your life to see if you still struggle with sin. If at that time you are still sinning, then He will announce, "He who is filthy, let him be filthy still." And if God doesn't see that you love Him enough to have stopped sinning, He will blot your name out of the book of life, and you won't be included in heaven. Probation for you will have closed.

By the time she was 14 years old she'd made up her mind. She couldn't possibly reach that level of perfection. In fact, she didn't think it possible. Because she couldn't possibly imagine a Deity that would make getting to heaven so hard, she concluded that there must not be a God at all.

Five years later when she was in college, she drove home on a Sabbath afternoon to surprise her family. Her car broke down about 45 minutes from home, so she used a pay phone and called her father. The response of her father, the faithful church member and employee of the church? "You know how I feel about you traveling on Sabbath. I'll come get you after sundown." She waited in her car for six hours until her father arrived—after the family had sundown worship without her.

Is that what doctrine is supposed to be? It seems as if some fall into the trap of letting it define them and their church instead of allowing their doctrine to describe our heavenly Father as lived out in the life, death, and resurrection of Jesus.

The challenge for the Seventh-day Adventist Church in the twenty-first century is to avoid employing doctrine to isolate ourselves. Rather, we need to make it clear that our doctrine portrays Jesus as the revealer of God's character. If our doctrine doesn't clarify a loving God as displayed by Jesus while He was on earth, we need to relook at our teachings.

Do we celebrate the Sabbath as a gift from God that finds its fulfillment in Jesus? Or do we use it to segregate ourselves from all those deceived people who have no idea that they live in Babylon? Has the Sabbath become our Messiah, or have we allowed the Messiah to become our Sabbath?

Once someone posted an article that circulated around the Seventh-day Adventist Church about former senator Joe Lieberman observing the seventh-day Sabbath. It heralded the fact that he knew the truth about the Sabbath.

Are you kidding me? Senator Lieberman doesn't believe in Jesus! What would the Sabbath be without Him? Observing the Sabbath and not believing in Jesus is tantamount to believing in the state of the dead without believing that Jesus will return and summon us out of our graves.

Our calling as a church is not to create a set of doctrines that will set us apart from a dying world. Instead, our doctrine should send us into a dying world that is starving for the truth about God as seen in Jesus!

I believe that each doctrine that our church holds dear is a wonderful revelation of God's character. At the same time I also fear that our church has sometimes yielded to the temptation to make our doctrines more about us than about our God. And I think that's one reason there are more ex-Seventh-day Adventists than active Seventh-day Adventists in the United States of America today.

We need to have strong biblical doctrines that reveal God as Jesus demonstrated Him in His life, death, and resurrection. And if we use our doctrine or teach it in any other way, for any other purpose, then we need to reexamine who we are as a church.

I love being a Seventh-day Adventist. I chose it on purpose. And I love what my church teaches about God.

A few years back I visited a man in the hospital. His whole family was there, and it looked as if he would experience a full recovery. I prayed with the family and then exited the room.

As I left, a nurse caught my attention. Quickly she told me that the elderly woman who occupied the next room over was on her deathbed and was very agitated. She saw that I was a pastor and wondered if I wouldn't just step in and talk with her.

As I walked into the room my eyes saw evidence of a once-vibrant woman who was barely a shell of her former self. Her body was so cancer-eaten that she could hardly shoulder her hospital gown.

Glancing up at me, she asked, "Who are you?"

I told her that I was a minister and that I had heard she was in some distress. I wondered if there was anything that I could do to help.

At first she told me that she didn't want to talk. Then, after we had chatted about some mundane things, she burst into tears. "I don't want to die and leave my husband!" she cried.

When I offered to call her husband or give him a ride to the hospital to sit with her, she shook her head. "You don't understand. My husband died 10 years ago. He's in hell, and I can't stand the thought of dying and going to be in heaven while he's down there suffering!" Her tears increased.

Now I understood. I could see why she was so upset. I would be if I were in her shoes too. "Do you mind if I show you some things in the Bible that might give you some different information about God?" I asked.

She acquiesced, and I was able to show her the beautiful picture of God in regard to death, hell, grace, and merciful judgment that the Bible reveals from cover to cover.

I'll never forget her response. "Wow! God is much better than I thought He was."

That sweet woman died in peace the very next morning.

Our doctrine comes from the Word of God. The Word of God testifies to His character as revealed in the life, death, and resurrection of Jesus Christ.

I fear that if we aren't careful, we could present our doctrine in ways that would have us end up looking like a lamb and sounding like a dragon. We find ourselves tempted to list our doctrines in some order that makes sense to us and employ them as points of information that we use to convince people about what's right. When we do this we start to draw lines in the theological sand separating ourselves from everyone who doesn't believe like we do.

I would submit that doctrine is not meant to separate, but to draw all humanity to the One who is the source of all true knowledge about God.

Do you want to know God? Know Jesus. Do you want a clearer picture of God? Study Jesus. Jesus is the doctrine of God.

CHAPTER **2**

Jesus the Follower

John the Baptist had become a huge attraction. People came in droves to see the evangelist prophet that ran around in the wilderness imploring people to repent of their sins and be baptized.

Because God blessed his ministry, John ended up with a bunch of disciples. They followed him around and learned from him. Ministering to his needs, they most likely hoped eventually to have a similar ministry.

And then one of John's disciples noticed something that the Baptist said about one of the people that came to be baptized by him. John studied the young man named Jesus and said, "Look, the Lamb of God who has come to take away the sins of the world!"

That statement startled John's disciples. They asked themselves what he could have meant by it.

But then the very next day John and his disciples saw Jesus again. Once more John announced Him as the Lamb of God, but this time he also told his disciples that when he had baptized Him, the Holy Spirit had anointed Jesus. John couldn't shut up about the Man.

And then John did something that nobody expected. "I must decrease, and He must increase," the Baptist announced.

John took the position of a follower.

Curiosity about this Jesus that John was saying all those things about was too much for two of John's disciples. They decided to follow Jesus to see who He was and where He was from. As they did so they asked, "Where do you live?"

Jesus' answer was simple: "Come and see."

One of John's disciples, a man named Andrew, spent that whole day in deep conversation with Jesus. And by the next morning he was convinced. He was no longer going to be a disciple of John's. Instead, he would now be a fully devoted follower of Jesus'.

In fact, he was so excited about who Jesus was that the next day when he was fishing with his brother, Andrew couldn't keep quiet about Jesus.

"As Jesus was walking beside the Sea of Galilee, he saw two brothers, Simon called Peter and his brother Andrew. They were casting a net into the lake, for they were fishermen. 'Come, follow me,' Jesus said, 'and I will send you out to fish for people.' At once they left their nets and followed him. Going on from there, he saw two other brothers, James son of Zebedee and his brother John. They were in a boat with their father Zebedee, preparing their nets. Jesus called them, and immediately they left the boat and their father and followed him" (Matt. 4:18-22).

Those three words would dramatically change the lives of dozens of people while Jesus was on earth, some for good and some, because of what they chose, for bad.

"Come, follow Me."

In his book *I Am a Follower* Len Sweet speaks of a dangerous trend in Christianity. One of the phenomena of the past 20 years in American Christianity is the sudden growth of mega churches. Tens of thousands of congregants fill stadium-like auditoriums to hear the words of very popular preacher/teachers.

The mega church movement has produced church leadership conventions, hundreds of books on Christian leadership, and itinerant preachers who train pastors in smaller churches in the art of leadership. The conventions have become popular events for people of all denominations. I've attended several of them. As for leadership itself, Andrews University has a doctorate program in it. Leadership and mentoring people into it so that we can have lots of leaders has become an obsession.

The summer camp applications and missionary applications I receive to fill out always have a question that asks me to rate the leadership skills of the applicant. Never once have I ever been asked on a reference form for any type of Christian ministry application to rate what kind of follower a person was. Never once.

Jesus said, "Come, follow Me."

I have searched through all the lists of spiritual gifts in Scripture, and do you know what I never find there? Leadership. It seems that we are not called to lead. Instead, God summons us to follow.

Again and again Jesus asks His friends to follow Him.

"Whoever serves me must follow me; and where I am, my servant also will be. My Father will honor the one who serves me" (John 12:26).

"He said to another man, 'Follow me.' But the man replied, 'Lord, first let me go and bury my father.' Jesus said to him, 'Let the dead bury their own dead, but you go and proclaim the kingdom of God.' Still another said, 'I will follow you, Lord; but first let me go back and say goodbye to my family.' Jesus replied, 'No one who puts his hand to the plow and looks back is fit for service in the kingdom of God' " (Luke 9:59-62).

"As he walked along, he saw Levi son of Alphaeus sitting at the tax collector's booth. 'Follow me,' Jesus told him, and Levi got up and followed him" (Mark 2:14).

"My sheep listen to my voice; I know them, and they follow me" (John 10:27).

"Whoever does not take up their cross and follow me is not worthy of me. Whoever finds their life will lose it, and whoever loses their life for my sake will find it" (Matt. 10:38, 39).

"As He was setting out on a journey, a man ran up to Him and knelt before Him, and asked Him, 'Good Teacher, what shall I do to inherit eternal life?' And Jesus said to him, 'Why do you call Me good? No one is good except God alone. You know the commandments, "Do not murder, Do not commit adultery, Do not steal, Do not bear false witness, Do not defraud, Honor your father and mother." ' And he said to Him, 'Teacher, I have kept all these things from my youth up.' Looking at him, Jesus felt a love for him and said to him, 'One thing you lack: go and sell all you possess and give to the poor, and you will have treasure in heaven; and come, follow Me' " (Mark 10:17-21, NASB).

Notice a pattern here? The overwhelming invitation we hear from Jesus in the Bible is "Follow Me." He never once says, "I've come to turn you into leaders"!

His invitation is for us to be followers. But in our day and age, who wants to be a follower?

In fact, even though people would tag Jesus as the greatest leader our world has ever known, He wasn't even a leader. He was Himself a follower.

"I don't do anything on My own, but what the Father tells Me to do," He said.

The reason Jesus was so very effective in His ministry here on earth was that He was a very good follower. As far as I can see in the Bible, every time a follower decided they wanted to take the lead in anything, it turned out to be a disaster. Adam and Eve, Abraham, Moses, King Saul, King David, King Solomon, Judas . . .

Not only is this true of Bible characters—I can tell you it's true in my own life.

I was at a camp meeting in New England and didn't have to speak on a Sunday until around 8:00 p.m. I had never been to Fenway Park to see the Green Monster, so I decided to run into Boston to watch the Red Sox play.

So, since it was Father's Day, I found a young man at the meetings who didn't have a father, and we journeyed into Boston to attend the game.

Now remember, this was before the days of GPS or cell phones that have that nice woman's voice that tells you when to take a left and a right. We got to the ballpark without getting lost, and enjoyed the game. After it we found a pizza joint. Then it was time to go.

Back in the car, I started to drive to where I thought the freeway back to Atlantic Union College campus was. But for some reason the road wasn't where I had remembered it to be. After about 20 minutes the young man looked at me and said, "Why don't you stop and ask for directions?"

Clearly he didn't understand what it takes to be a man. Men don't need directions. Men blaze a trail. They are leaders, not followers.

After another 30 minutes I was more lost then ever. Finally I had to admit that if I didn't get some sort of directions, I was going to be late to my meeting that night.

So I stopped at a gas station and asked. Those directions took me on another 30-minute journey deeper into the city. In fact, I think I passed that gas station three times while searching for the on-ramp.

Finally I got a bright idea. Spotting a taxicab sitting on the side of the road, I pulled over, got out of the car, and knocked on the driver's window. I handed him $10 and said, "Can you let me follow you to the freeway on-ramp so that I can get back to Lancaster?"

In less than five minutes I was on the freeway.

Following the right person can really make a difference in your life.

Jesus looked at His disciples and said, "Come, follow Me." I want you to notice what Jesus was asking here.

When a rabbi invited a young man to follow him, Jewish society considered it an extreme privilege, because only the best and the brightest got such an invitation. Every child would attempt to memorize the Torah by an early age. By the age of 12 they would then try to learn the rest of the Old Testament.

After memorizing the Holy Writings, a student would approach a rabbi and ask them if they could be their student. The rabbi would interview them, and then, if the student was not up to snuff, he would announce, "Go and ply your trade." In other words, "Sorry, kid, but you aren't good enough to be in my school." At that point the saddened student would go back home and be a fisherman, or a carpenter, or a tax collector.

If, though, the student was good enough, the rabbi would tell him, "Come, follow me!" At this point the student would return home to say goodbye to his family. And the mother and father would recite, "May the dust of your rabbi completely cover you." In other words: "May you follow him so closely that you are covered in his dust."

Notice how Jesus did things differently here. His disciples didn't come to Him asking for an interview. Instead, He went to them with the invitation.

And pay attention to whom He approached. Jesus found people who were already plying their trade and invited them to follow Him. They were all the guys who were not the cream of the crop. In fact, as time went on, He got accused of hanging around sinners, drunks, and tax collectors.

Jesus picks ordinary average Joes to be on His team.

"Come, follow Me."

Notice furthermore how everybody that decided to follow Jesus had to give up something in order to do so. Peter, Andrew, James, and John had to abandon their fishing nets. Matthew had to leave his tax table. Mary had to stop being a prostitute. The rich young ruler had to sacrifice his wealth. Jesus challenged the Pharisees to discard their religion if they wanted to follow Him.

In each case, whenever people encountered Jesus there was a call to follow Him, but usually it came at a cost.

"Anyone who loves their father or mother more than me is not worthy of me; anyone who loves their son or daughter more than me is not worthy of me. Whoever does not take up their cross and follow me is not worthy of me. Whoever finds their life will lose it, and whoever loses their life for my sake will find it" (Matt. 10:37-39).

There always seems to be a cost to following. But that is true about whomever we choose to pursue.

All kinds of voices beg for our attention; all kinds of people try to get us to follow them.

Maybe I'm old, but the whole Twitter deal does not appeal to me. I've had friends in ministry tell me I should open a Twitter account and see how many followers I could get. That seems so unbiblical to me!

I don't want followers—I want to be a follower.

Today everybody desires to be a leader. Everybody seeks followers. One talk radio host calls his fans "Ditto Heads." Another one labels them his "Drones."

People on TV want you to follow them. Everyone from the fashion world to the religious world is looking for adherents.

And in the midst of all the noise from this world we have a Savior who approaches us with a still small voice and beckons us, "Come, follow Me." He won't yell louder than all the other voices, but the call will be persistent.

"Come, follow Me."

When we respond to His invitation to follow, we choose to walk with Him, to drink from His cup, to eat at His table. Jesus' invitation is consistent. Always and forever it will be "Follow Me."

It was His first invitation to Peter as he was mending his nets on the seashore that first day. And in the end, after three and a half years of ministry together, after all Peter's victories and failures, it was the last invitation Jesus gave him.

In John 21 Jesus invites the disciple to love Him and feed His sheep. Getting distracted, Peter starts to ask Him about the fate of another disciple, but Jesus, sensing Peter's struggle, pulls his attention back to the task at hand and says, "Peter, follow Me."

This is still Jesus' call to you and to me. Follow Me.

It's not an easy decision. To follow Jesus may mean I have to give up something so that I can respond to the invitation. It may mean I need to stop taking the lead in my own life and start to follow. Or it may require that I shift my attention from other things that I am perusing so that I can truly follow Jesus.

Revelation 14:4 describes God's last-day people: "These are those who did not defile themselves with women, for they remained virgins. They follow the Lamb wherever he goes."

The invitation is clear. Jesus chooses you. He's standing in front of you right now, and He's saying, "Come, follow Me."

CHAPTER 3

Jesus and the Law

One of the great realities of life has to do with where laws come from. Usually they result from human behavior that we think needs to be curtailed or at least modified.

Another way to put it is like this: Laws get created when people are walking along and see someone doing something that is kind of gross or at least unsafe, and they say, "You know, there ought to be a law against that."

When I was the principal in Wenatchee, Washington, our school shared a parking lot with the church. At one place in that shared parking lot the distance between the church and the gymnasium is about 25 feet. That part of the church has a flat roof that is only about eight feet from the pavement.

For years that roof sat there unnoticed. Nobody thought of it. And then one day some teachers saw a small group of students on top of the roof playing tag.

In response they created a law: No climbing on the roof. Before the students climbed on the roof a law was not needed. Now there's a sign on the wall just below the ledge of the roof. That sign is law.

When we read the laws in the Old Testament, it's not hard to see why they came into being. For thousands of years God's people had been doing things that were harmful to their bodies, to one another, and to their understanding of God. So somebody said, "There oughta be a law." That somebody was God.

He announced laws about stealing, murder, adultery, making idols, and reserving time for rest on the Sabbath. Israel also received laws about becoming clean or unclean because of what they touched or ate. God gave His people laws about how to treat slaves and poor people. What to do with a bull that gored someone walking through a pasture. Whom they could sleep in the same bed with and what to do when someone was unhappy in a marriage.

God's people actually ended up with 613 laws. That's a lot. And it seemed that nobody was ever able to obey them perfectly. As hard as they tried, at some point everybody found themselves lacking when it came to being a perfect law keeper.

Now remember, a Jew wasn't just responsible for obeying the Ten Commandments. They had to keep all 613 laws. When the Bible refers to "the law," it has in mind all 613 laws found in the first five books of the Bible, not just the Ten Commandments.

The Ten Commandments are relatively easy to obey, if one sticks to the letter of the law. It's not been hard not to murder people or steal their things. I don't have to struggle with not committing adultery or honoring my father and mother. I like my father and mother!

Now, tangle those 10 minimum requirements up with 603 other laws, and things start to get complicated.

As I have studied the 613 laws of the Torah, I had to ask the questions: How did Jesus relate to and abide by the law? Did He obey all 613 perfectly?

Before I answer them, I'd like to ask you a question: Did God give the law to Israel to bring them closer to Him and one another, or was the law given just to be kept no matter the circumstance? In other words, what's its purpose?

When I was in seventh grade, my class had some behavioral problems. In a nutshell, we were all acting like a bunch of seventh graders. One day I guess we were all particularly squirrely, and our English teacher, Mrs. Johnson, had had enough.

She slammed a book down on her desk and yelled, "The next person to say any word is going to get swats! Now do your worksheets!" For the next 30 minutes you could have heard a pin drop.

And then, just before the bell for class to get over rang, the girl next to me, Kelli Peisley, accidentally knocked some papers and her book off the top of her desk.

Leaning down, I picked them up for her and handed them back.

She quietly said, "Thank you."

I barely audibly replied, "You're welcome."

"MARK WITAS! GET DOWN TO THE OFFICE! YOU ARE GOING TO GET SWATS!"

I was marched down to the office where the law was restated (no talking or else there would be swats), the evidence was presented (Mrs. Johnson had witnessed that I had talked) and the verdict was rendered (swats from Mr. Busby would be provided). And they were—vigorously.

I broke the law. But did I do the right thing? What was more important, the law or the action that violated it? Perhaps I should have quoted Scripture to her: "For I desire mercy, not sacrifice, and acknowledgment of God rather than burnt offerings" (Hosea 6:6).

As I've studied Jesus' relationship with the law I have come to some startling realizations—at least for me.

You see, I had always been under the impression that my salvation was somehow tied up in how Jesus came to earth as a human being and obeyed all 613 points of the law perfectly. I've always thought that Jesus' perfect law keeping was God's standard for His Son so that He could somehow credit us with His perfect obedience and we could then be saved and go to heaven.

But after studying the life of Jesus in regard to law keeping, I think I have a different impression of His relationship to the law than I used to. Let me explain.

The law says that if you touch a dead person, you are to be unclean for a week. No contact with anybody for seven days. While you have to go through some water purification rituals, you are still unclean for a week. No exceptions to the rule.

"Whoever touches a human corpse will be unclean for seven days. They must purify themselves with the water on the third day and on the seventh day; then they will be clean. But if they do not purify themselves on the third and seventh days, they will not be clean. If they fail to purify themselves after touching a human corpse, they defile the Lord's tabernacle. They must be cut off from Israel. Because the water of cleansing has not been sprinkled on them, they are unclean; their uncleanness remains on them" (Num. 19:11-13).

That is the law. But Jesus decided to ignore the letter of the law for the good of the person. He touched a dead girl to raise her to life again. But the law doesn't give a prevision for this. It just says if you touch a dead person you are unclean.

Consider another Old Testament law: "If they unwittingly touch anything ceremonially unclean (whether the carcass of an unclean animal, wild or domestic, or of any unclean creature that moves along the ground) and they are unaware that they have become unclean, but then they come to realize their guilt; or if they touch human uncleanness (anything that would make them unclean) even though they are unaware of it, but then they learn of it and realize their guilt" (Lev. 5:2, 3).

Jesus ignored that law on several occasions in order to heal lepers.

And then there is the law that Jesus rescued the woman caught in adultery (see John 8). She had been apprehended in the very act. Her accusers had enough witnesses as required by the law. And the penalty was unwavering: "If a man is found sleeping with another man's wife, both the man who slept with her and the woman must die" (Deut. 22:22). "If a man commits adultery with another man's wife—with the wife of his neighbor—both the adulterer and the adulteress are to be put to death" (Lev. 20:10).

Jesus' opponents present Him with the opportunity to hold up the letter of the law. The law gives no room for repentance to save the life of the adulterer. The penalty is death. Yet Jesus decides that the letter of the law is not appropriate here. Instead, He chooses mercy and redemption.

On another occasion, as Jesus and His disciples walked through a field, the disciples gathered food from the crop and ate it. The problem was that it was Sabbath.

The law is clear. Given as the response to an incident in Israel's history, it plainly declares that people are not to go out and gather food to eat on the Sabbath. "Nevertheless, some of the people went out on the seventh day to gather it, but they found none. Then the Lord said to Moses, 'How long will you refuse to keep my commands and my instructions? Bear in mind that the Lord has given you the Sabbath; that is why on the sixth day he gives you bread for two days. Everyone is to stay where he is on the seventh day; no one is to go out.' So the people rested on the seventh day" (Ex. 16:27-30).

The Pharisees were right according to the letter of the law when they accused Jesus' disciples of breaking the Sabbath regulation. But how did He respond?

"Jesus answered them, 'Have you never read what David did when he and his companions were hungry? He entered the house of God, and taking the consecrated bread, he ate what is lawful only for priests to eat. And he also gave some to his companions.' Then Jesus said to them, 'The Son of Man is Lord of the Sabbath' " (Luke 6:3-5).

Jesus defended His disciples by giving a precedent of another law that King David had broken. Accused of breaking the law, He cited another time that someone violated the law and got away with it.

And finally Jesus threw the religious leaders all in a tizzy because He was healing on Sabbath. While nothing in the law that says that you can't do that on the Sabbath, why couldn't He have found a way to do it on a Sunday or a Wednesday and avoid the controversy?

What's interesting to me is Jesus' reaction to their accusations. "Jesus said to them, 'My Father is always at his work to this very day, and I too am working' " (John 5:1).

Notice that Jesus doesn't say, "Well, healing people really doesn't constitute work . . ." Nor does He try to tell the religious leaders that what He is doing isn't breaking the Sabbath. He says, "Yeah, I'm working today, on the Sabbath. So is My Father. What are you going to do about it?"

What I discovered from Jesus as I studied His relationship to the law is that God provided the law for His children to aid them in coming closer to

Him and to one another. The letter of the law doesn't always guarantee this, but its spirit certainly does.

When asked His opinion about the greatest law of all, Jesus said, " 'Love the Lord your God with all your heart and with all your soul and with all your mind.' This is the first and greatest commandment. And the second is like it: 'Love your neighbor as yourself.' All the Law and the Prophets hang on these two commandments" (Matt. 22:37-40).

You see, God designed the law to aid us in loving and serving Him and in loving and serving humanity in a deeper and more powerful way.

The founding prophet of our church knew this. In *Christ's Object Lessons* Ellen White writes that "God's law is the transcript of His character. It embodies the principles of His kingdom. He who refuses to accept these principles is placing himself outside the channel where God's blessings flow" (p. 305).

If you were to sum up God's character in one word, what would you choose? Would you choose the word "law"? No, you would most likely say "love." The principle of the law is What is the most loving thing I can do in a situation? We ask ourselves, "How can my actions most reflect God's love to the people around me? How can what I do best show God my love toward Him?"

Sometimes that principle of love would have us abide by the letter of the law. And other times we may find ourselves breaking all kinds of laws in an emergency to get our loved one to the hospital as quickly as possible.

It was the principle of love that caused Jesus to ignore the letter of the law and touch the leper and dead people. The principle of love had Jesus overlook the letter of the law as His disciples gathered food to eat on the Sabbath. And the principle of love led Him to bypass the letter of the law and grant mercy to the woman caught in adultery.

Our Savior did all these things because He knows full well that you can't have a relationship with rules. He realizes that the law can save no one. "Knowing that a man is not justified by the works of the law, but by the faith of Jesus Christ, even we have believed in Jesus Christ, that we might be justified by the faith of Christ, and not by the works of the law: for by the works of the law shall no flesh be justified" (Gal. 2:16, KJV).

Jesus understood that the law was a framework for the children of Israel to guide them in getting along with one another and to enable them to stay close to God. But Jesus also recognized that the law falls woefully short in many kingdom matters. It can't save or love. Nor can you have a relationship with it.

That's why He actually turned the law on its head when He quoted it as saying, "An eye for an eye, and a tooth for a tooth." And then added, "But I say to you, turn your cheek, love your enemy, and pray for those who persecute you."

The law does not teach these things, but they follow the principle of love and God's character as the letter of the law cannot do.

When we stick to the letter of the law as Christians, we can sometimes become less like God and more like tablets of stone. Ellen White saw it happening to the Seventh-day Adventist Church, and in 1888 she mourned, "As a people, we have preached the law until we are as dry as the hills of Gilboa that had neither dew nor rain. We must preach Christ in the law."

You see, our first duty is to love as God does. Our first duty is to act as Jesus would. And our high calling is to reveal God's loving character to a world that doesn't need another law. But they do need a picture of a loving God that they can put their trust in and have a relationship with.

God does not summon us to hold up and promote tablets of stone, but to reveal His character by lifting up Jesus, who said, "When I be lifted up I will draw all men to Me" (See John 12:32).

As we view our religion from this paradigm, everything changes. The Sabbath isn't a moral law or a commandment written on stone anymore. Now the Sabbath becomes a chance to deepen our relationship with God and to do things for our fellow human beings that will display the divine character in attractive ways.

By seeing the law as Jesus did, we allow God to take the tablets of stone and the letters on parchment and place them in our hearts as expressions of love for Him and for one another.

When we become this kind of people, when God can plant His law in our hearts so deeply that our lives become a reflection of His character . . . that's when things become interesting.

CHAPTER **4**

Jesus and the Churches

This time, instead of looking at Jesus from one of the four Gospels, I want to study Him as He speaks to His church through the book of Revelation.

In Revelation 2 and 3 Jesus communicates to seven churches a message that essentially declares, "Hold on. Don't give up. Stand firm. Overcome."

Each of the seven churches has some good things about them that Jesus really admires. And, as you might guess, each of them also have some things that they are doing or have stopped doing that He would like to see changed.

Many theologians would say that these seven churches represent different eras in Christianity down through the Middle Ages and until now, and that Laodicea would represent the twenty-first-century church in North America and Europe.

While this may be true, I would remind all of us that each of those churches were real, going through real persecution. It came from both outside and from inside the church. The internal persecution resulted from people who decided that compromise was OK.

The seven letters to those seven churches dealt with real congregations with real people that were under real distress. For them, worshipping Jesus was oftentimes a matter involving life and death.

So Jesus writes them letters. And at the end of each letter He places a promise. He says that if believers would stand to the end and overcome, they would receive wonderful rewards:

- They would be able to eat from the tree of life.
- They would receive crowns of life instead of the second death.
- They would eat hidden manna, receive a white stone, and be given a new name.
- They would receive the morning star.
- They would wear white garments and their names would not be blotted out of the book of life.
- They would be pillars in God's temple and receive His name.
- They would sit on the throne with Jesus.

People who endured severe persecution from the Roman Empire for their faith would receive each of those promised things. All of those faithful believers were longing for Jesus to come again. Many were resigned to the notion that it was likely that they would end up either perishing because of their faith, or dying from old age. And always they lived with the knowledge that they might face death just because they wanted to worship Jesus.

I love the promises listed at the end of the letters to the seven churches. They symbolize all that every believer hopes for as they live in this ugly world and look forward to their soon redemption.

To the church of Ephesus, Revelation 2:7 announces, "To him who overcomes, I will grant to eat of the tree of life which is in the Paradise of God" (NASB).

The tree of life is a scriptural image that holds great meaning and a certain amount of wonder. It's something that symbolizes life without end. The Bible doesn't mention it much, but we do have some clues as to the significance of it in a few different texts.

Genesis 3:22 says, "Then the Lord God said, 'Behold, the man has become like one of Us, knowing good and evil; and now, he might stretch out his hand, and take also from the tree of life, and eat, and live forever' " (NASB).

Evidently the fruit on the tree of life was so powerful that it gave mortal human beings the ability to be ageless and never die. I'll bet that fruit tastes really good. Jesus promises those who overcome, even if their standing for truth ends in death, an opportunity to eat that juicy, life-giving fruit.

I look forward to the taste of that fruit, but maybe there is more here than just the promise of not dying. Being that the book of Revelation is highly symbolic, maybe eating from the tree of life is also a metaphor that would suggest something more than the physical act of consuming fruit.

Proverbs 3:18 says, "She is a tree of life to those who take hold of her, and happy are all who hold her fast" (NASB). Proverbs 11:30 adds, "The fruit of the righteous is a tree of life, and he who is wise wins souls" (NASB). And then Proverbs 13:12 promises, "Hope deferred makes the heart sick, but desire fulfilled is a tree of life" (NASB).

The book of Proverbs associates the tree of life with fulfilled desires and a life of joy and final satisfaction. Maybe the promise to those who overcome means that, when it's all said and done, if we stand up for the right, if we remain faithful to Jesus, if we don't give up no matter what life throws at us, we will in the end have our every desire fulfilled. In the end we will be satisfied. And in the end we will have everlasting joy.

To the church in Smyrna, Revelation 2:10, 11 promises, "Be faithful until death, and I will give you the crown of life. . . . He who overcomes shall not be hurt by the second death" (NKJV).

James 1:12 adds, "Blessed is a man who perseveres under trial; for once he has been approved, he will receive the crown of life which the Lord has promised to those who love Him" (NASB).

The assurance of a crown of life for those who overcome is a special promise too. A crown signifies authority. When we overcome this world and stay faithful to Jesus, sin has no power over us any longer. Because we stand in Him, God gives us final authority over the wages of sin, because Jesus has final authority over sin. In case you haven't figured it out, this is very good news for us.

To the people of the church in Pergamum, Revelation 2:17 declares, "To him who overcomes, to him I will give some of the hidden manna, and I will give him a white stone, and a new name written on the stone which no one knows but he who receives it" (NASB).

I want to focus on both the white stone and the new name here for a moment. First the whole idea of receiving a new name . . .

I find it interesting that the Bible associates a person's name with their character or their destiny. Notice, for example, the times that God changed people's names in the Bible. Jacob had his name (destiny or character) changed from Jacob (meaning "one who supplants" or "deceiver") to Israel (many translate that as "Prince of God").

Abraham had his name transformed from Abram ("exalted father") to Abraham ("father of many"). His name altered when his destiny changed with the covenant of circumcision and the promise of God.

Both acquired new names after they struggled with God in this life and received a new destiny. As their characters changed, they obtained their new name. God promises us a new name as we practice the overcoming life. Our new life will be rooted in the fact that we will now display the true character of God.

I also find it interesting that those new names will be written on stone. If names in the Bible are synonymous with character, ask yourself a question. Is there any other time in the Bible when someone's character gets inscribed on stone?

You guessed it. God placed His character on stone when He wrote with His own finger on the tablets that made up the Ten Commandments. It would seem that those who overcome will have a new name, and that name will be His name transcribed on our hearts.

So why a white stone? Some argue that the white stone held up by a judge during trail signified a full acquittal. Proponents of that interpretation would say that the white stone is Jesus' declaration to us of "Not Guilty!"

Other scholars have noted that it may allude to the practice in certain pagan religions of people carrying an amulet or stone with the name of their deity inscribed on it. Supposedly they used them as a source of magical power. To know the name of a deity was to have a claim upon his or her aid.

Of all the ideas of what a white stone could point to, I think my favorite is that the ancients often employed white stones as tokens of membership or tickets for right of entry to community festivals. If that is the background for the text, the white stone may symbolize the saint's right of entry to the feast of Revelation 19.

To those in Thyatira, Revelation 2:26-28 pledges, "He who overcomes, and he who keeps My deeds until the end, to him I will give authority over the nations; and he shall rule them with a rod of iron, as the vessels of the potter are broken to pieces, as I also have received authority from My Father; and I will give him the morning star" (NASB).

Second Peter 1:19 says, "So we have the prophetic word made more sure, to which you do well to pay attention as to a lamp shining in a dark place, until the day dawns and the morning star arises in your hearts" (NASB).

And Revelation 22:16 adds, "I, Jesus, have sent My angel to testify to you these things in the churches. I am the Root and the Offspring of David, the Bright and Morning Star" (NKJV).

The question here isn't what the morning star is—it's *who* the morning star is. The morning star is Jesus. And Jesus is the one who shines the light of understanding on His people. He illuminates the true nature and character of God through His followers. Our reward for being overcomers is to know God because we know Jesus.

To the church of Sardis, Jesus says in Revelation 3:5, "He who overcomes will thus be clothed in white garments; and I will not erase his name from the book of life, and I will confess his name before My Father and before His angels" (NASB).

Our ultimate reward here is to have our name remain in the book of life. As we read Scripture we understand that everyone's name is included from the beginning. But because of their actions or because of their desire to shun God's graces, some will actually get blotted out of the book of life, not because the Lord wants to, but because some will actually not desire to have anything to do with God.

The author of Psalm 69:28 pleads, "May they be blotted out of the book of life and may they not be recorded with the righteous" (NASB). Interesting here is the "they" that David wants removed from the book of life are the enemies of God and His anointed. Have you ever wondered what God's enemies are doing with their names in the book of life?

And then Philippians 4:3 adds, "Indeed, true companion, I ask you also to help these women who have shared my struggle in the cause of the gospel, together with Clement also and the rest of my fellow workers, whose names are in the book of life" (NASB).

Consider the texts here. The book of life includes both God's enemies and His friends. Evidently God's enemies hadn't yet pushed the Holy Spirit away so that they would be erased from that book.

In other words, we aren't born lost with the task of someday doing something to persuade God to put our names in the book of life. We are born saved (with a sinful nature) with the choice to accept the gift of our salvation or ultimately reject it and ask God to erase our name from the book.

I think it's important here to understand that the battle Satan has waged over your soul isn't one to get you to do something wrong. Rather, it is for your mind. He is trying to do anything he can to get you to give up on God, to throw in the towel, to make you think that maybe He doesn't even exist. The devil wants to fill you with apathy and discouragement. And if he can't get you to stop believing in God, than he'll try to get you so angry at Him that you would rather curse Him than bless Him.

The battle for your soul is on. But to him who overcomes . . . his name will never be blotted out of the book of life.

The Jesus promise to the faithful in Philadelphia appears in Revelation 3:12: "He who overcomes, I will make him a pillar in the temple of My God, and he will not go out from it anymore; and I will write upon him the name of My God, and the name of the city of My God, the new Jerusalem, which comes down out of heaven from My God, and My new name" (NASB).

To be a pillar in the temple of God . . . wow. In my opinion it isn't talking about a future heavenly temple. Remember, the New Jerusalem has neither a temple nor a need for one, because God Himself will be our temple. Jesus is talking about being a firmly established part of the body of Christ, one who can be strong and depended on. Overcomers are people who stand firm in the faith.

And one more thing: Did you notice that not only are we going to get a new name, but so is Jesus? I wonder what that name will be.

And finally Laodicea. In Revelation 3:21 Jesus says, "He who overcomes,

I will grant to him to sit down with Me on My throne, as I also overcame and sat down with My Father on His throne" (NASB).

Again, this is all metaphorical. I'm pretty sure that we won't sit on an actual throne with God as His equal. But what does the victory of a believer signify here? To sit on a throne is to rule over something.

When we overcome on this earth we rule over sin, death, and condemnation. Yet in reality, it's not us, but Christ in us that establishes our dominion. "Therefore, there is now no condemnation for those who are in Christ Jesus" (Rom. 8:1). These are the rewards for those who stay true to Jesus, even through the tough times.

The verses in the book of Revelation that we have looked at often conjure up thoughts of the future. We've taken the book and placed it in the category of the not yet—something that is going to happen in days of persecution and times of trouble yet to come.

These letters to the seven churches were written to real people who were going through real challenges in the real world.

Overcoming isn't something that happens only in the future—it's taking place right now. And our reward for overcoming isn't just something that awaits us someday. We can experience the rewards of overcoming in the here and now.

Nor are we just going to be under attack from the evil one sometime in the future. He wants dominion over us right now and is doing his best to discourage us and take us out of the game every moment. The devil is doing everything he can to distract us with the glitz and glamour of this world. Constantly he tries to take our attention off of Jesus and put it on things that will one day fade away. Satan seeks to shift our priority away from a relationship with Jesus to one with whatever trouble he has shuttled into our lives.

The work of overcoming isn't a future work—it's what we must do now.

Revelation 2:10, 11 call us to be "faithful until death, and I will give you the crown of life. . . . He who overcomes shall not be hurt by the second death" (NASB).

In other words, our trials on this earth may be things that we cannot be delivered from . . . at least not now. They may even result in death, a temporary state of sleep. But that's not the end. Because if we remain faithful, even to the point of death—if we overcome, even to the point of breathing our last on this earth—then the second death will have no power over us.

If we remain faithful to the end, then we will hear that last trumpet call and Jesus will raise us imperishable and we will see our Savior face to face.

As I write this chapter I've found myself in and out of the hospital visiting Londa Raines, one of my elders and a wonderful Christian woman who is battling cancer. When I visit with her I go away from that room, every time, knowing that I am visiting an overcomer.

At one point, when things were looking pretty dire, we talked about dying and funerals and things that pastors and parishioners discuss when events aren't going to turn out too good. I chased everyone out of the room, and then Londa and I talked. And the whole time we did, all Londa could do was bless the Lord for all the things that He had done for her in her life. No tears. No regrets. Nothing negative to say. Just praise.

Londa realizes that her battle with cancer may end in death. But she has chosen to be an overcomer . . . and a fighter, for that matter. She's a tough little cookie.

You see, this is the attitude and the mind of Christ. Satan is going to do his best to knock us down, and he may have our body, but we don't have to give up our hearts and minds to the discouragements of the evil one. Our minds and our souls belong to Jesus.

Jesus' message to the people of the seven churches—His message to you and me—is not to give up. Stay the course. Run the race, and both on this earth and on the earth to come we will receive our reward.

CHAPTER 5

Why Jesus Came

A few years back I went on a mission trip to Mexico that was probably the most physically arduous workout experience I've ever had.

The long driveway leading to the orphanage we were working at had some pretty bad water damage from erosion. What it needed was about a quarter-mile trench dug on each side of the driveway to drain the rainwater away. Each trench had to be about two feet deep and about two and a half feet wide.

The ground was hard, and shovels were just not adequate for the job. We had to use picks and metal bars to loosen the ground.

It was hot, sweaty, and dirty work. But everybody was putting in great effort except one girl. It seemed as if every time I glanced up Allison was on a break, walking around looking lost or smelling a flower. Finally I started to hear some grumbling about her laziness.

Pulling Allison aside, I asked her to help a little more. She stared at me and said, "I don't want to. I don't like to work like that."

"Well, then, how about helping the housemothers with the orphans?"

"I don't want to do that, either. I don't like having to be in the house with all those noisy kids."

Out of mere frustration I finally blurted out, "Allison, why did you come down here? Why are you on this mission trip?"

She looked at me blankly and said, "I really don't know."

There is nothing more frustrating than not knowing why we are where we are.

Not having a purpose in life can leave a person feeling lost and disoriented.

Conversely, if someone knows who they are, where they are supposed to be, and what they should be doing there, they usually enjoy a gratifying and empowering feeling.

Since I've been a pastor I've had numerous people ask me, "Why did Jesus have to come to earth?" or "Why did Jesus have to die?"

First of all, let's be clear: Jesus didn't have to come to our world—He wanted to. It was His desire to do what He did.

Second, I have heard all kinds of reasons people think Jesus came. For example:

- He came to die for my sins.
- He came so that I can go to heaven.
- He came to show us that it's possible to keep the Ten Commandments.
- He came because God needed somebody to die to satisfy His law so that He could save us.

All of these reasons are filled with possibilities and problems. And Christians have offered all of them at one time or another.

But if you are really going to try to answer the question of why Jesus came to earth, wouldn't it be a good idea to go right to the horse's mouth?

If I lived during His time and were to walk up to Him and ask, "Hey, Jesus! Why are You here? What's Your big purpose in life?" what would His answer be?

Well, we're in luck. Jesus had several occasions in which He actually answered our question for us. Some of those answers appear word for word from one Gospel to another, so, for purposes of brevity, if Matthew, Mark, Luke, and John repeat them, I'll just cite one passage.

I've divided Jesus' purpose for being on earth into nine categories. (I suppose one could have consolidated them into fewer categories, but I arranged them into nine.) So here's the list—the things Jesus said He was here to do:

1. To fulfill the law. "Do not think that I came to abolish the Law or the Prophets; I did not come to abolish but to fulfill" (Matt. 5:17, NASB).

2. To call sinners/lost people. "But go and learn what this means, 'I desire compassion, and not sacrifice,' for I did not come to call the righteous, but sinners" (Matt. 9:13, NASB).

3. To create division. "Do not think that I came to bring peace on the earth; I did not come to bring peace, but a sword. For I came to set a man against his father, and a daughter against her mother, and a daughter-in-law against her mother-in-law" (Matt. 10:34, 35, NASB).

4. To serve/give His life as a ransom. "Just as the Son of Man did not come to be served, but to serve, and to give His life a ransom for many" (Matt. 20:28, NASB).

5. To preach the kingdom of God. "But He said to them, 'I must preach the kingdom of God to the other cities also, for I was sent for this purpose' " (Luke 4:43, NASB).

6. To save lives. "For the Son of Man did not come to destroy men's lives, but to save them" (Luke 9:56, NASB). "For God did not send the Son into the world to judge the world, but that the world should be saved through Him" (John 3:17, NASB). "For the Son of Man has come to save that which was lost" (Matt. 18:11, NASB).

7. To cast fire on the earth. "I have come to cast fire upon the earth; and how I wish it were already kindled!" (Luke 12:49, NASB).

8. To do the will of the Father. "For I have come down from heaven, not

to do My own will, but the will of Him who sent Me" (John 6:38, NASB).

9. To tell the truth. "Therefore Pilate said to Him, 'So You are a king?' Jesus answered, 'You say correctly that I am a king. For this I have been born, and for this I have come into the world, to testify to the truth. Everyone who is of the truth hears My voice'" (John 18:37, NASB).

So Jesus offered nine different reasons for being here. That's not surprising, is it? After all, who of us couldn't think of several reasons God has us on earth?

I know that He put me here to be a father, a husband, a preacher, a teacher, a friend, and a truthteller. All of those purposes carry equal weight in my allotted time here on earth. And all of them are God-given ones that I am to take seriously each time I am called to carry out one of those roles.

To somehow rank the several goals that God has for me on this earth would be difficult, wouldn't it? And I don't think that's something that we could even do with Jesus' purposes on earth. Every objective that He had was important and deserves our attention as we study the "why" of Jesus.

I'd like to look at just three of the above nine in more detail: to preach the kingdom of God, to create division, and to save lives.

The first reason Jesus came to earth that I'd like to talk about was to preach the kingdom of God. "But He said to them, 'I must preach the kingdom of God to the other cities also, for I was sent for this purpose'" (Luke 4:43, NASB).

Jesus used the phrase "kingdom of God" more than 50 times in the gospels. He seemed to be bent on explaining it to His listeners. He told parables about the kingdom, said that certain people would be a part of it, and that by their actions and attitudes other people could not enter into the kingdom of God.

Jesus said some very disconcerting things about the kingdom, such as that it belongs to children and to people who think and act like children, but not so much to the rich and arrogant.

Elsewhere He compared the kingdom of God to a person who sows seeds and to a mustard seed.

So what is the kingdom of God? Where is it? What does it look like?

Most people assume that the kingdom of God is in heaven. That it's something that will happen for us in the future. We consider ourselves to be far from the kingdom of God while we are still on earth. But that's not how Jesus pictured or preached it. Interestingly, His idea of the kingdom is a real combination of the now and the not yet.

Yes, some elements of the kingdom of God do seem yet future. "Truly I say to you, I will never again drink of the fruit of the vine until that day when I drink it new in the kingdom of God" (Mark 14:25, NASB). The expression "that day" in the New Testament usually refers to a time post Second Coming. So Jesus envisioned that the kingdom would happen for sure sometime in His and our futures.

I've often wondered what the look on Jesus' face is going to be like when we are all around that humongous banquet table and He tastes the juice of the grape for the first time again in thousands of years. I'll bet after He drinks a big gulp of it He will wipe the grape juice mustache off with His sleeve and exclaim, "I've really missed this!"

While there is indeed an element of the kingdom of God that yet is future, at the same time we must be careful as believers that we don't somehow only relegate it to that. Because the kingdom of God is also in the right now. Consider these texts that talk about it in a different timeframe:

"But if I cast out demons by the Spirit of God, then the kingdom of God has come upon you" (Matt. 12:28, NASB).

"Has come" is past tense, isn't it? The kingdom of God was right there in Israel, because Jesus was right there in Israel. Wherever Jesus is, there is the kingdom of God.

"Now having been questioned by the Pharisees as to when the kingdom of God was coming, He answered them and said, 'The kingdom of God is not coming with signs to be observed; nor will they say, "Look, here it is!" or, "There it is!" For behold, the kingdom of God is in your midst' " (Luke 17:20, 21, NASB).

Jesus is the kingdom of God. Wherever He is, there will be the kingdom. But the kingdom is still here on earth, right now. Did you know that?

"Therefore I say to you, the kingdom of God will be taken away from you and given to a people, producing the fruit of it" (Matt. 21:43, NASB).

When Jesus said this, He was talking to the leaders of Israel, who were supposed to be doing kingdom work, but instead were shredding the character of God by misrepresenting Him in how poorly they treated people. Instead of being a light on a hill they separated themselves from the world. The salt of the earth had lost its saltiness and was now only good for the dunghill.

Then when the religious leadership drug Stephen out and stoned him, a transition happened. The kingdom of God transferred to a new nation, a holy priesthood of men and women who believed in Jesus Christ.

The kingdom of God on earth is what happens when a whole bunch of people become new creations and then come together to worship the King of their kingdom.

You see, the kingdom of God isn't a place. It's an attitude or mind-set. So you won't find it on some map of the universe. The kingdom of God consists of kingdom citizens, and we encounter kingdom citizens both all over the globe and in heaven.

At one point in Jesus' ministry a teacher of the law, a Pharisee, posed a question to Him. "Which law is the greatest of all?" he asked.

"Love God with your everything, and love your neighbor as yourself," Jesus answered. When the Pharisee agreed, Jesus then said something remarkable. "When Jesus saw that he had answered intelligently, He said to him, 'You are not far from the kingdom of God' " (Mark 12:34, NASB).

Jesus wasn't speaking about miles or kilometers. He was talking about understanding and practice. When a person loves the Lord with everything they've got and loves their fellow citizens in that same tangible way, they are living in the kingdom of God. And they are also advancing it.

So Jesus' purpose on earth was to preach about what it would look like to live in the kingdom of God. At the same time He also showed us how to live out the kingdom of God on earth.

The second reason Jesus came to earth that I'd like to consider was to create division. "Do not think that I came to bring peace on the earth; I did not come to bring peace, but a sword. For I came to set a man against his father, and a daughter against her mother, and a daughter-in-law against her mother-in-law" (Matt. 10:34, 35, NASB).

The Gospels record just a few of these kinds of statements. And it used to be that every time I read one of them I'd get a weird feeling in my stomach about it. But then I realized that when groups of people start embracing kingdom life, living it out on earth right here and now, it will cause others to react.

The kingdom of God is revolutionary. Not how we do things around here, it flies in the face of the prince of this world and his plans for how he wants things to be.

One day as Peter and John walked in the Temple area in Jerusalem they came upon a man who had been born without the ability to walk. All his life friends and family had had to carry him to a place where he could beg for enough money to eat every day.

As Peter and John passed by, the man asked for some money. The two disciples hadn't worked in three and a half years, so they didn't have any. But since they did reside in the kingdom of God, they took a detour from wherever they were heading and healed the lame man. The man who could not walk before now did. He jumped and leaped and praised God.

And for healing someone and doing kingdom work, Peter and John got arrested and flogged.

Doing kingdom work in Jesus' name is divisive. It pits families against each other. Not only did Jesus fully realize that God had sent Him to invite people into the kingdom—He was equally aware that that kingdom, even though its members acted peacefully, would sometimes cause division and even violent persecution.

The last purpose for Jesus on earth I'd like to examine was His mission to save lives. "For the Son of Man did not come to destroy men's lives, but to save them" (Luke 9:56, NASB). John 3:17 adds: "For God did not send the Son into the world to judge the world, but that the world should be saved through Him" (NASB). And Matthew 18:11 declares, "For the Son of Man has come to save that which was lost" (NASB).

A lot of people equate being saved with being helped. When someone helps you, you have been getting along OK until now but just need a little something more, and someone then gives you a hand.

But Jesus didn't come to our world to help me. He entered it to save me. The big question is: to save me from what?

I have a friend who went to her doctor because she had flu symptoms. During that exam the doctor discovered a lump that, if it had gone undiscovered, could have ended up taking her life. I remember her expression as she said, "Getting the flu probably saved my life!"

And what does Jesus save us from? He saves from death—the wages of sin; the wrath of the dragon.

You see, the dragon hijacked our world back in the Garden of Eden. And since then he has swung humanity around by the tail. He has set his claim over Adam and Eve and all of their children.

Jesus came to rescue us from the wages of our sin. By canceling the debt that it hung on us, He made void Satan's claim over you and me.

And just like my friend who had the flu, we may have noticed symptoms of being lost, but we didn't know the severity of our disease until the Great Physician touched us with His healing touch.

When Jesus heals us, He invites us into the kingdom of God—not someday in a land fairer than gold, but right now. Right now He asks us to extend the kingdom to one another on this earth. He invites us into kingdom living.

When we agree to live kingdom lives, people won't understand. They may even get hostile when we turn our backs on sin and start living peaceful lives of obedience and joy. But radical kingdom-of-God living will make a difference in this world. And when lived with purpose, it will draw other men and women into kingdom living.

Daniel 2 says that the kingdom of God will grow and grow and grow until it fills the whole earth. We have the privilege of being agents in spreading the kingdom and in helping it to expand.

Jesus will come back and reclaim those who have chosen kingdom life. And the kingdom life that started here with the likes of you and I will one day be located on a new earth. No longer will there be a division between the now and the not yet. The not yet will be the now. And we will live with the King of our kingdom face to face, forever and ever.

CHAPTER 6

Jesus Touched

Jesus and His disciples had just sailed back from across the Sea of Galilee to a huge crowd of people waiting to greet Him. Word had spread of His arrival, and the vast throng wanted to get close to Him—to sit at His feet and learn about the kingdom of God. They hadn't heard anyone speak like this before.

A large group also came with physical ailments. They had heard that Jesus had made the blind see, the lame walk, and the mute speak. The crowd pressed in until one voice stood out in the crowd above the others.

"Jesus! Please! Please, Jesus! I need your help!"

When Jesus looked down, He saw Jairus prostrate at His feet. The man was on the pastoral staff at a local church and appeared to be in distress. The crowd stopped for a moment, trying not to trample the man lying at Jesus' feet.

"Jesus! My daughter, she's very ill, to the point of death! Jesus, she's my only daughter. Is there something you can do?"

Immediately Jesus helped the man to his feet and said, "Take Me to her."

The crowd seemed to press in just a little tighter now. The disciples were on their guard, trying to protect their Master.

Have you ever been in a situation in which a crowd made you feel almost claustrophobic?

When Wendy, my wife, and I were in Ukraine doing an evangelistic series, we had to travel during the day on public buses. We'd get into one when it was three-fourths full and watch as at each stop more people would surge in. It was 100 degrees, and the buses had no air-conditioning. Each time we'd conclude that the vehicle couldn't possibly hold another person, 20 more would squeeze on.

A couple times some of the young people on our trip could lift their feet up off the floor and not fall. The crowd was so pressed in that one of our girls actually fainted but remained upright.

That is what I imagine the crowd around Jesus was like on the day He walked down the street to Jairus' house.

It was in the mad rush and confusion of that crushing mob that Jesus stopped abruptly and appeared about to say something. Now, when He paused to speak, it was kind of like those old E. F. Hutton commercials. Do you remember them? When E. F. Hutton spoke, people listened. And when Jesus stopped to speak, people also paid attention.

Jesus stood in the middle of that massive crowd and said something that His disciples deemed ridiculous. "Who touched Me?"

James looked at Him and said, "You're kidding, right?"

Peter chimed in, "Uh, everybody touched You. It's kind of thick with people here."

And Thomas commented, "I highly doubt anybody touched You."

"I know somebody touched Me, because power went out of Me." I wonder what that would have felt like. Was it a sudden lack of energy? Or was it like someone rubbing their feet on the carpet and then shocking you with a touch?

His eyes searched the flock of sheep that so desperately craved a Shepherd. One of His lambs had touched Him, and He wasn't going to continue down that street until He knew who it was.

"Who touched Me?"

Finally a woman stepped forward and confessed. A constant bleeding had tormented her for so many years that it drove her to try to get close enough to Jesus that she might have a chance at being made whole.

In a desperate attempt to be made well she found the courage despite her anemic condition to fight through the crowd toward Jesus. Being knocked down still again by the packed throng, she reached out with one final attempt to just touch the Master.

As she lunged at Him, she caught just the hem of His garment. Just one touch. But she felt strength fill her body. Her cheeks flushed for the first time in a decade. She knew that that touch had done the trick—knew that she was healed.

Jesus confirmed what she already knew. "Daughter, your faith has healed you."

Touch. It's such a powerful thing, isn't it? Psychologists who have studied it have figured out how important touch is to long-term intimate relationships, such as marriage.

One psychologist suggests 12 progressive steps that lead to intimate relationships. The first three don't involve touch. They are:

1. Eye to body (seeing someone across a room)
2. Eye to eye (the first time your eyes meet)
3. Voice to voice (the first time you talk to each other)

The next nine all have to do with touch:

4. Hand to hand
5. Hand to shoulder
6. Hand to waist

7. Face to face (kissing, hugging)

8. Hand to head (This might seem as if it's out of place, but when was the last time you ran your hand through someone's hair who wasn't intimate on some level with you?)

The Christian world reserves the last four steps for a marriage relationship.

9. Hand to body

10. Mouth to breast

11. Touching below the waist

12. Intercourse.

Now, the interesting thing about the list is what researchers concluded about touch and the kinds of touch involved in the 12 steps:

1. In this day and age many people rush through steps 1-8 (or skip many of them altogether) so that they can get to steps 9-12, or what's called sexual intimacy. When people do this, their relationship is more likely to fail than if they take time in progressing through steps 1-8 on a longer road to mature intimacy.

2. Even more interesting is that couples that maintain a long-lasting and intimate friendship—good marriages—continue to share steps 4-8 and don't forget those meaningful touches. Couples that have happy and meaningful relationships will still hold hands, put their arm around each other, and fiddle with each other's hair.

Human touch plays an important role in long-term relationships. It also has the power to heal.

Psychologists John Bowlby and René Spitz separately studied orphaned infants during World War II. In their studies infants held, cuddled, and otherwise loved with human touch thrived in eastern European orphanages. But they noted that infants that were cared for without human touch and nurture would actually become sickly and even die.

In a New York *Times* article by Daniel Goleman entitled "The Experience of Touch: Research Points to a Critical Role," he reported that premature infants massaged for 15 minutes three times a day gained weight 47 percent faster than others left alone in their incubators—the usual practice in the past. "The massaged infants also showed signs that the nervous system was maturing more rapidly." As a result "they became more active than the other babies and more responsive to such things as a face or a rattle."

"The massaged infants did not eat more than the others," Tiffany Field, a psychologist at the University of Miami Medical School who did the study, said. "Their weight gain seems due to the effect of contact on their metabolism."

Massaged infants got discharged from the hospital an average of six days earlier than premature infants not massaged, saving about $3,000 each in hospital costs, Field noted.

"Eight months later, long after their discharge, the massaged infants did better than the infants who were not on tests of mental and motor ability and held on to their advantage in weight, according to a report by Field in *The Journal of Pediatrics*."

"The standard policy in caring for premature infants has been a minimal-touch rule," she said. Word of her continuing findings and others that support them has led to a change in policy in many hospitals.

Neonatal wards previously kept babies born prematurely in incubators and fed them intravenously. Nursing staff touched them as little as possible because they had observed the infants becoming agitated when someone approached or handled them. The agitation sometimes put a dangerous strain on their tiny lungs, putting them in danger of hypoxia, an inability to oxygenate the blood.

"However, Field found that a light massage of the babies' backs, legs, and necks and gentle movement of their arms and legs proved to have a tonic effect, immediately soothing them and eventually speeding their growth."

All these dramatic changes in such babies happened simply from touch.

In a study intended to discover why Americans seem to be more and more disconnected from one another sociologists sought to determine if the problem in society is simply the result of the electronic age, or if something else was going on.

Sidney Jourard decided to do a worldwide study on intimacy among couples in a public setting. What he did was set up hidden observation posts in cafés around the world to observe friends as they ate and talked with each other. What he discovered was interesting.

Couples in a café in Puerto Rico touched 180 times, in an hour while they sat in a coffee shop together. Those in Paris did so 110 times in an hour. But couples in the United States touched two times in the hour. And in Great Britain they touched zero times in an hour.

His study correlated with others that measured the health of relationships in those countries. Countries that didn't inhibit public touch had healthier and more meaningful familial relationships than those that inhibited touch.

Touch is such a powerful thing.

Another study conducted an experiment on trust and touch. It asked people to invite perfect strangers to engage in activities that would be helpful. When a light touch to the arm or shoulder accompanied the invitation, the person was much more likely to participate than if they were just merely asked.

Touch is powerful. Touch is persuasive. And touch is healing.

Jesus touched people. All through Scripture we find Him touching people and often in significant ways.

One day when Jesus was leaving Jericho, He heard the loud calls of two blind men asking for mercy. Stopping, He spoke with them. When they asked if He would heal them, "Jesus had compassion on them and touched their eyes. Immediately they received their sight and followed him" (Matt. 20:34).

Another time, when He visited Peter and his family, the disciple's mother-in-law became sick. Matthew 8:15 tells us that "he touched her hand and the fever left her, and she got up and began to wait on him."

And I love this example of Jesus' touch. Matthew 8:1-3 reports that "when Jesus came down from the mountainside, large crowds followed him. A man with leprosy came and knelt before him and said, 'Lord, if you are willing, you can make me clean.' Jesus reached out his hand and touched the man. 'I am willing,' he said. 'Be clean!' Immediately he was cleansed of his leprosy."

Nobody had touched the leprous man for years. I'm convinced that when Jesus did so, the power of that touch was not just a physical power that healed. It communicated love and trust and intimacy that the man hadn't felt since he had been first declared unclean. Jesus touched people that desperately needed it. I also believe that He has given us this same opportunity. If we are to be good at our high calling to reveal the loving character of God to our world, we need to touch people in the name of Jesus.

Recently I heard a sermon by my colleague Randy Roberts. In it he suggested that many of us in the church need to have Jesus touch us not once, but twice.

The Bible recounts a blind man who asks Jesus to heal Him. It's one of those stories that I didn't understand until recently when I heard Randy talk about Jesus' second touch.

Mark 8:22-25 recounts Jesus' healing of a blind man at Bethsaida. Some people brought the man to Him and begged Jesus to touch him. "He took the blind man by the hand and led him outside the village. When he had spit on the man's eyes and put his hands on him, Jesus asked, 'Do you see anything?' [The man] looked up and said, 'I see people; they look like trees walking around' " (verses 23, 24). Once more Jesus put His hands on the man's eyes. Then his sight was fully restored, and he saw everything clearly. It was Jesus' second touch that brought the man to the place he needed to be, so that he could be whole.

Jesus' initial touch brought us to the place of conversion. At that time we pledged our life to Him and told Him that we would serve Him for the rest of our lives.

But that was a long time ago. I think a lot of us now need that second touch from Him. It's not that we have backslidden or rebelled against God, but rather that we've just lost our passion for Him. We need that second touch to open our eyes to the needs of those around us so that we, in turn, can be the touch of Jesus in this world.

CHAPTER 7

Jesus' Teaching on the Mount: The Lord's Prayer

When I was a college chaplain and associate pastor at Canadian Union College, some church members came by regularly. In all actuality I'm not sure that they ever had anything specific in mind—they just wanted to come into my office, that of the senior pastor, or into the office of one of the other associates, just to express their concerns.

One individual gained a reputation as someone who would sit and talk for a half hour or more without really saying anything. But it was difficult for me to pay attention. I found my mind wandering to all the things I should be doing. But in the interest of being polite, and knowing that the person needed to have someone to talk to, I'd sit and listen. Sometimes by the end of our conversation I'd go through the exercise of trying to figure out what my visitor had actually said. The church member always seemed to want something, but whatever it was changed at least three times during the conversation.

Many words, no content.

During the Sermon on the Mount Jesus addressed the topic of speaking to God through prayer. He said that it's wrong to think that God will hear us because we babble on like the pagans who assume that their deities will pay attention because of their many words.

When you are writing a paper for your teacher, it's often important to check your word count so that you have the required minimum words to get your A. Not so with prayer. Prayer is to be a meaningful conversation in which words matter. Jesus gives us an example of how directed our conversation with God can be. We call it the Lord's Prayer.

Now, I don't know about you, but there are certain scriptures that I've memorized that I feel can be recited only in the language of the King James Version. The twenty-third psalm, John 3:16, and the Lord's Prayer are three of them.

Let's look at the Lord's Prayer as Jesus taught it to His disciples: "Our Father which art in heaven, Hallowed be thy name. Thy kingdom come. Thy will be done in earth, as it is in heaven. Give us this day our daily bread. And forgive us our debts, as we forgive our debtors. And lead us not into temptation, but deliver us from evil: For thine is the kingdom, and the power, and the glory, for ever. Amen" (Matt. 6:9-13, KJV).

It's interesting that the church has taken this prayer and made it a part of its liturgy. In actuality, Jesus wasn't asking His followers to memorize and repeat it a whole bunch of times. He was just giving an example of how to pray. He said, "This, then, is how you should pray . . . Here is an example of directed prayer." Jesus was teaching His followers how to have a conversation with the Father.

I'm not saying we shouldn't repeat the Lord's Prayer. I think it's beautiful. But I do believe that if we repeat the Lord's Prayer and don't mean every word of it with our hearts, we are just babbling like the pagans who think their gods will hear them just because of their many words.

So if this is a directed prayer, I'd like to take a look at its elements and hopefully apply them to our prayer lives.

Our Father which art in heaven . . .

The very introduction to the prayer tells us a lot. Jesus called the God of the universe His Father. In fact, in this prayer He refers to Him as "our" Father.

Now when some people think of a father, they have warm thoughts of a loving daddy who provided love and support for them in their lives. They remember a warm embrace and a strong example of a healthy mix of discipline and love.

But others may freeze up. They may have memories of rage and abuse, fear and neglect.

Ellen White wrote an article about raising children that she published in the December 18, 1900, *Review and Herald*. In it she said something that is both sobering and enlightening. It's just one little line that sums it all up: "Parents stand in the place of God to their children."

If that is the case, and I'm sure it is, can you see how so many young people grow up either fearing or disrespecting God as their Father?

I have had students that were so angry at God that they ignored Him because of the abuse they had suffered at the hands of their human father. They had projected onto God what their father had done to them.

As parents we have the divine responsibility to live balanced, godly lives as we interact with our children—not to earn God's love, but to give our children a true look at a loving Father in heaven.

When Jesus suggested that we address God as "Our Father who art in heaven," He wasn't thinking of the Father as a stern dictator or an irresponsible and undependable man of the house. He visualized Him in terms of a daddy. In Mark 14:36 Jesus calls His Father "Abba" Father. Abba was a term of familiar affection that a child would have for a loving parent. When we address our Father in heaven, we need to remember that He is our loving daddy.

Romans 8:15 tells us: "The Spirit you received does not make you slaves, so that you live in fear again; rather, the Spirit you received brought about your adoption to sonship. And by him we cry, 'Abba, Father.'"

Galatians 4:4-6 adds: "But when the set time had fully come, God sent his Son, born of a woman, born under law, to redeem those under the law, that we might receive adoption to sonship. Because you are his sons, God sent the Spirit of his Son into our hearts, the Spirit who calls out, 'Abba, Father.'"

Some may still have in their lives a warped perception of what a father should be. That's not your fault. But take comfort in this: Our Father in heaven is every bit of the daddy that you may have never had. He's our Abba Father, and you can address Him that way with the kind of childlike innocence and wonder that will not be denied by the One who taught us that we need to approach the kingdom of God as little children.

God is our Abba Father, and we can take comfort in that and address Him as such.

Hallowed be thy name . . .

What is God's name? When Moses asked the Lord to give him a name to take back to the Israelites, what was the Lord's answer? "And God said unto Moses, I AM THAT I AM: and he said, Thus shalt thou say unto the children of Israel, I AM hath sent me unto you" (Ex. 3:14, KJV).

Do you think that's really God's name, or do you think He was telling Moses something?

I was listening to talk radio not too long ago and heard a story about a teacher that had a student in their classroom named Nosmo. The teacher asked the child where he got his name, but the lad had no clue. Finally, during parent-teacher conferences the teacher asked the child's mother where she had obtained the name Nosmo. The child's parents had the last name of King. She said they couldn't figure out a name for the birth certificate, so they looked around the room and saw a no smoking sign. Their last name was "King," so Nosmo it was.

In order to have a name, someone needs to give you one. Usually the person to name something or someone is either its creator or its procreator. People who invent something often label it after themselves. People who procreate name their children.

Who can name God? He is not created or invented. He just is. So when Jesus says "hallowed be thy name," what name is He talking about?

When the Bible uses the word "name" it's often synonymous with the word "character" or "essence."

After ancient Israel began writing down the name of God, they eventually stopped reading it out loud. Today, we would pronounce that name "Yahweh." But ancient Hebrew culture substituted the vowels of another name, because they considered "Yahweh" too holy.

The Greek word for holy is *agios,* defined as "set apart or sacred to God; make holy, consecrate; regard as sacred; purify, cleanse." As Jesus teaches His disciples to pray, He reminds them that He is our Abba Father, but that Abba Father is above and beyond anything we can imagine. Our Abba Father is the one and only Creator of the universe. Our Abba Father is holy. Hallowed be Thy name.

Thy kingdom come . . .

Ever since Jesus came to earth, the desire of every believer is that God establish His kingdom on earth and end the pain and suffering associated with our sin-sick world. Every believer desires to be reunited with family members who died. Every believer wants to receive the gift of eternal life on the earth made new. And every believer longs to see Jesus face to face.

The Seventh-day Adventist Church originated out of this deep desire. When William Miller discovered the time prophecy and did the math of Daniel 8:14, the first Adventist Christians banked everything on the date when they expected Jesus to return. They couldn't wait to see their Savior! And when He did not come October 22, 1844, it devastated them.

"Our fondest hopes and expectations were blasted, and such a spirit of weeping came over us as I never experienced before," Hiram Edson wrote. "It seemed that the loss of all earthly friends could have been no comparison. We wept, and wept, till the day dawn."

Was it because they were embarrassed that Jesus didn't come when they had predicted? Was it because they didn't want to have to remain here on earth anymore? Was it even because they weren't reunited with their deceased loved ones? No, it was because they longed for God's kingdom to come.

That desire became so intense among the early Advent believers that they included it in our name. We are Seventh-day Adventists, because we long for the Second Advent to end this world of sin, and we long to see the kingdom of God set up with all of its promises fulfilled. Our very name says "Thy kingdom come!" Thy kingdom come is in our very DNA.

Thy will be done, on earth as it is in heaven . . .

This sentence reminds us that we need the "Thy kingdom come" to happen. We understand that God's will is done in heaven, but we also recognize that His will does not always take place on earth.

When my mom got a brain tumor, I was just a teenager. I remember one of the church elders coming to me in the hospital and saying something to the effect of "sometimes it's really hard to know why things happen, but we know that if they happen, it is God's will." Really? It was God's will for my mother to get a brain tumor?

We see events in our sin-sick world that are anything but God's will. And as a consequence, two Bible verses don't let us forget that things on earth are not always going to go how God wants them to:

"The highest heavens belong to the Lord, but the earth he has given to mankind" (Ps. 115:16).

"I have seen something else under the sun: The race is not to the swift or the battle to the strong, nor does food come to the wise or wealth to the brilliant or favor to the learned; but time and chance happen to them all" (Eccl. 9:11).

God's will does not always get done on earth. But we do have the opportunity to give Him permission to have His will fulfilled in our lives. We can live the kind of lives that will reflect His will for us in this world. And though we may have to suffer the results of things in the present world that are not His will, we are able to live through the pain with God in our hearts and by our side. Our prayer should be that God live out His will in us.

Give us this day our daily bread . . .

It's interesting that Jesus would include in this prayer a request from us to Abba Father to take care of our basic needs. Why would a loving Father need His child to ask for bread before He gave it to him?

I think Jesus understands that it is healthy for us to recognize that God is the provider of all we have. One of the reasons that we bow our heads and thank God for our food is because it is good for us to acknowledge His blessings in our life. I don't like it that some have gotten into the habit of asking God to "bless" the food they are about to eat instead of thanking Him for it. Because God gave you that food, He's already blessed it. But in an act of remembering that He is God and that He is the provider, when we thank Him for the food we are recognizing that all is His and not ours.

We can say the same about the money we have. When was the last time you thanked God for the funds He has given you? When was the last time you recognized that He is the God of your money and has blessed you with it?

We bow our heads and thank God for our food each time we eat. But when was the last time we bowed our heads as a family and thanked God for our paycheck that we've received so that we could buy food to eat?

As we acknowledge God as provider, we treat what He has provided us more sacredly, and maybe share those blessings (food and money) more liberally and responsibly than we would otherwise.

And forgive us our debts, as we forgive our debtors . . .

This is by far one of the most unpopular texts in the Bible. We like the concept of forgiveness. But we are uncomfortable with the idea that the forgiveness we receive from God is limited to the forgiveness we extend to others.

One of the most frightening texts in Scripture appears just after the Lord's Prayer: "For if you forgive other people when they sin against you, your heavenly Father will also forgive you. But if you do not forgive others their sins, your Father will not forgive your sins" (Matt. 6:14, 15).

I've had people tell me, "God wouldn't do that to me! That's not how He is!"

I guess the question I would have for such a person is Why would God (or anyone else, for that matter) want to be in heaven for eternity with someone who would willingly choose to harbor bitterness in their hearts?

Have you ever met somebody that was just not able to let go and forgive? It's been said that not forgiving someone is like trying to kill the rodents in your house by drinking the rat poison yourself.

Forgive us your debts *as we forgive our debtors.*

And lead us not into temptation, but deliver us from evil . . .

This part of Jesus' example of how to pray has also caused some consternation among God's people. Why would the Lord lead me into temptation? In fact, it seems to fly directly in the face of James 1:13: "When tempted, no one should say, 'God is tempting me.' For God cannot be tempted by evil, nor does he tempt anyone."

The word here translated "temptation" (*peirasmos*) is usually translated as "trial" or "test," as in James 1:2. The Greek here is a permissive imperative. The idea is Do not allow us to be led into temptation. In other words, this part of our prayer is to ask God to guard our lives from the kinds of things that will distract us from a meaningful relationship with Him. It's almost asking Him to protect us from the dumb decisions that we sometimes make for ourselves that get us into all kinds of trouble.

In a way, it is a prayer not just to God but also to ourselves. If we are going to ask Him not to allow us to be led into temptation, we need to do our part to avoid it.

A farmer once saw a little boy lying under one of his apple trees looking at the ripe fruit. The man yelled out, "Boy, are you stealing my apples?"

The boy, gazing upward, replied, "No, sir. I'm trying not to!"

For thine is the kingdom, and the power, and the glory, for ever. Amen.

We should note that the most reliable manuscripts don't have this part of the Lord's Prayer in them. Yet enough of them do so that some translations still carry it as a part of the passage.

Whether added later or whether Jesus said it Himself doesn't really matter to me. It's still an important element of prayer, because it points to God's sovereignty. The phrase acknowledges that God is God and we are not. Thine is the kingdom, Thine is the power, and Thine is the glory forever!

I have no kingdom, I have only the power God has given me, and I claim no glory, because it is all His.

This part of the prayer also points forward to a time when the redeemed of God will stand on a sea of glass mixed with fire in front of the throne of God. "And I saw what looked like a sea of glass glowing with fire and, standing beside the sea, those who had been victorious over the beast and his image and over the number of his name. They held harps given them by God and sang the song of God's servant Moses and of the Lamb: 'Great and marvelous are your deeds, Lord God Almighty. Just and true are your ways, King of the nations. Who will not fear you, Lord, and bring glory to your name? For you alone are holy. All nations will come and worship before you, for your righteous acts have been revealed' " (Rev. 15:2-4)

Thine is the kingdom, and the power, and the glory forever! I'm looking forward to singing that song with the saints, aren't you?

CHAPTER **8**

I was only a year into being baptized into my local Seventh-day Adventist church and wanted to propose to my girlfriend, Wendy. But I had noticed that she didn't wear any kind of jewelry. What should I do?

One of my friends who had been an Adventist all his life told me that among those who didn't want to wear jewelry, many people gave an engagement watch to their fiancés. So I bought a watch.

I'll never forget the night that I asked Wendy to marry me. The two of us were sitting down at a Mexican restaurant in Lynnwood, Washington, enjoying our favorite meal. We had been going out only for about a month and a half.

When something distracted her attention for a moment, I slid the watch box in front of her plate. It took her a second to see it, but when she did, she looked at it, glanced at me, stared back at it, then faced me and started crying.

First she said yes! Then no. Finally, "Yes, but with some conditions."

Conditions? What conditions?

I had to pass her parents' inspection. A daunting task, to be sure. And I had to drive to her hometown and consider living there someday.

Well, I knew all about her hometown. After all, she couldn't stop talking about it. I recognized that someday soon I was going to have to make the drive to Bella Coola, British Columbia. What I didn't fully comprehend was that the route to Bella Coola included about 200 miles of dirt road. *Two hundred miles of dirt road!* Nor did I realize that a part of the road was really only one lane wide, at an 18 percent grade, with a 1,000-foot drop on one side and a rugged rock wall on the other.

We started on our 14-hour journey early one summer morning. Eleven hours later we were going down switchbacks made for donkeys, not cars. It was the only time I had the sensation of being at a carnival while I was in my car. Occasionally big trucks hurtled up the road as I traveled down it. We had to squeeze way over to let them by, our mirror almost scraping the side of the passing vehicle.

But once we got down in the valley we were able to see the most beautiful of God's creation. In short, at the end of the road was a mountain paradise that rivals any place on earth for its beauty and grandeur.

I loved it so much that I ended up living in the Bella Coola Valley for the next four years of my life as the boy's dean and Bible teacher at the academy there. Sometimes, if you are willing to take it, the difficult road can lead you to a better place.

Robert Frost wrote one of the most famous poems in American literature.

Two roads diverged in a yellow wood,
And sorry I could not travel both
And be one traveler, long I stood
And looked down one as far as I could
To where it bent in the undergrowth;

Then took the other, as just as fair,
And having perhaps the better claim,
Because it was grassy and wanted wear;
Though as for that the passing there
Had worn them really about the same,

And both that morning equally lay
In leaves no step had trodden black.
Oh, I kept the first for another day!
Yet knowing how way leads on to way,
I doubted if I should ever come back.

I shall be telling this with a sigh
Somewhere ages and ages hence:
Two roads diverged in a wood, and I—
I took the one less traveled by,
And that has made all the difference.

In Matthew 7:13, 14 Jesus says, "Enter through the narrow gate. For wide is the gate and broad is the road that leads to destruction, and many enter through it. But small is the gate and narrow the road that leads to life, and only a few find it."

For years I've heard this verse used to reference all kinds of things that pastors and authors have supposed the "narrow gate" or "the narrow road" to be.

Some have seen keeping Sabbath as walking down the narrow road, while others say that believing the right doctrines is the way to enter through the narrow gate. People have attributed all kinds of things to the narrow way.

But when we are honest with the context of Scripture and let Jesus speak for Himself, we find that the narrow way is something different than those things. In fact, it is linked to doing what Jesus says in verse 12. "Do to others what you would have them do to you." That is the narrow way. To extend grace when you can just as easily disperse justice is the narrow way. To judge people as you would want to be judged is the narrow way. The narrow way is Jesus' way.

But to take a small liberty with this text, I would like to say that the narrow way is more than just Jesus' method of relating to the human beings around us. The narrow way is Jesus. Period.

"Therefore Jesus said again, 'Very truly I tell you, I am the gate for the sheep. All who have come before me are thieves and robbers, but the sheep have not listened to them. I am the gate; whoever enters through me will be saved. They will come in and go out, and find pasture. The thief comes only to steal and kill and destroy; I have come that they may have life, and have it to the full' " (John 10:7-10).

Jesus is the gate. And He wants us to walk through that gate and allow Him to be the Shepherd of our lives. Walking the narrow way is to walk as Jesus did. It's to follow the path of a servant/follower and not a master/leader.

The Last Supper was Jesus' final attempt before His crucifixion to bring unity to His followers through a demonstration of servanthood.

In John 13 He demonstrated to His disciples what it looked like to walk through that narrow gate:

"It was just before the Passover Festival. Jesus knew that the hour had come for him to leave this world and go to the Father. Having loved his own who were in the world, he loved them to the end. The evening meal was in progress, and the devil had already prompted Judas, the son of Simon Iscariot, to betray Jesus. Jesus knew that the Father had put all things under his power, and that he had come from God and was returning to God; so he got up from the meal, took off his outer clothing, and wrapped a towel around his waist. After that, he poured water into a basin and began to wash his disciples' feet, drying them with the towel that was wrapped around him. He came to Simon Peter, who said to him, 'Lord, are you going to wash my feet?' Jesus replied, 'You do not realize now what I am doing, but later you will understand.' 'No,' said Peter, 'you shall never wash my feet.' Jesus answered, 'Unless I wash you, you have no part with me.' 'Then, Lord,' Simon Peter replied, 'not just my feet but my hands and my head as well!' Jesus answered, 'Those who have had a bath need only to wash their feet; their whole body is clean. And you are clean, though not every one of you.' For he knew who was going to betray him, and that was why he said not every one was clean. When he had finished washing their feet, he put on his clothes and returned to his place. 'Do you understand what I have done for you?' he asked them. 'You call me "Teacher" and "Lord," and rightly so, for that is what I am. Now that I, your Lord and Teacher, have washed your feet, you also should wash one another's feet. I have set you an example that you should do as I have done for you. Very truly I tell you, no servant is greater than his master, nor is a messenger greater than the one who sent him. Now that you know these things, you will be blessed if you do them'" (verses 1-17).

It was really the most amazing display of the narrow gate that Jesus could have shown His disciples short of the cross. But it's also really hard to comprehend, isn't it?

Here is the kind of narrow gate life that Jesus has called us to demonstrate with our families, our coworkers, our church members, and our world. Jesus is the narrow way.

CHAPTER 9

All day Jesus had been teaching about the kingdom of God. And all day He had been healing and caring for people and holding little children who wanted His blessings. By now He had established a following that numbered in the hundreds—people who flocked to Him, met His needs, and hung on His every word.

When evening came He announced that He wanted to travel to the other side of the lake. The disciples and other followers prepared several boats for the journey, and they set sail. Exhausted from the day, Jesus found a cushion in the back of one of the boats and lay down. The gentle rocking of the boat soon sent Him into a deep sleep.

As He slept, the wind picked up and the waves started to toss the little fleet about until it began to worry some of the experienced sailors. Then, when the wind turned into gales that drove water over the edge of the boats, the disciples started to fear for their lives. They had no life jackets or lifeboats. But the disciples, in their fear, did realize that there was a Life-giver on board.

One of the fearful followers stumbled to the back of the rocking vessel and shook Jesus awake. "Jesus! Don't you even care if we drown?"

Rubbing His tired eyes, Jesus stood and looked around at the frightened and soggy disciples and spoke. "Peace, be still."

"Then the wind died down and it was completely calm" (Mark 4:39).

Jesus made peace. He was a peacemaker.

"Blessed are the peacemakers, for they shall be called the sons of God" (Matt. 5:9, NKJV).

What exactly does it mean to be a peacemaker? I'd love to have the ability to stand out on my deck during a rain and windstorm and say, "Peace, be still!" and have it actually work. Now, I haven't tried that yet, but I'm relatively sure that it wouldn't make much of a difference.

Again, what does it mean to be a peacemaker?

Parents of little children know a little about what it means to be a peacemaker, don't they? So do elementary school teachers. Every day parents and teachers find themselves in the business of helping little ones resolve their conflicts so that they can have peace.

When I was little, my sister and I were pretty much always in conflict. I would egg her on until she was just crazy with anger. She'd scream and yell and throw things, and I'd aggravate her some more.

The only thing that kept the peace in our home was the threat of my dad or mom walking in and taking matters into their own hands. Both of them could leave a mark on our behinds, so if we knew they were around, we'd keep our conflict to a minimum.

One day, my sister got so mad that she threw a jar of jam at me. I ducked and the jar hit the back of our couch, tearing a hole in the back of it.

As soon as we saw that, the conflict stopped. My sister and I realized that our mother would soon come home from work, so we rapidly rearranged the furniture so that the back of the couch was against the wall.

Mom didn't find out about the hole for several years.

My mom was a peacemaker. Not so much because she had great negotiating skills—more because she carried a mean paddle.

The scene in the Temple was anything but peaceful. The money changers, the cattle, the sheep had so filled the Temple courts with commerce that a person hoping for a moment of peace with their God there would be sore out of luck.

Jesus took in that scene like my mom would of if she would have walked in with my sister and I screaming at each other. He made a whip and started swinging it around until the Temple courts were clear and peace reigned again.

Sometimes we have to create the peace through a little thunder and lightning, don't we? In fact, as we read the book of Revelation, we see that in this old world we aren't going to have peace until we go through some pretty significant turbulence.

I think it's important to say here that this kind of peacemaking, one that results from a little bit of fear and intimidation, should rarely happen. If you look at the totality of Jesus' ministry, His "peacemaking" had little to do with fear and much to do with love.

I'm guessing that when Jesus said, "Blessed are the peacemakers," that that wasn't a call to arms . . . it was more a summons to be conflict resolvers.

So how do I become a peacemaker?

A call for peace implies that conflict already exists. The question is, What do you do when there is conflict? Do you add to it? Or do you try to create peace?

One sure way to get things more riled up than they are is to add to the fray by gossiping about the situation. "Without wood a fire goes out; without a gossip a quarrel dies down" (Prov. 26:20).

Oh, we love gossip, don't we? Isn't it great to have the inside scoop when nobody around you does? And don't we love to share the juicy parts of a story that nobody else may be privy to?

It's a top money-making industry. While real newspapers are losing money and folding from city to city, tabloids and gossip rags continue to make millions.

Have you ever been the victim of gossip? At one time in our lives my family has. And even though some of the things said about me or my family may have been true, the gossip that traveled around the community of believers that we lived in made it very difficult to move on from the conflict we were trying to heal from.

Gossip created anything but peace in our lives.

"Furthermore, just as they did not think it worthwhile to retain the knowledge of God, so God gave them over to a depraved mind, so that they do what ought not to be done. They have become filled with every kind of wickedness, evil, greed and depravity. They are full of envy, murder, strife, deceit and malice. They are gossips, slanderers, God-haters, insolent, arrogant and boastful; they invent ways of doing evil; they disobey their parents; they have no understanding, no fidelity, no love, no mercy" (Rom. 1:28-31).

Paul says that people who gossip are filled with every kind of evil and depravity. Gossipers are not peacemakers and shall not be called the children of God.

We had a cook in a boarding school that I worked in named Anne Astleford. I once had a juicy bit of gossip to share with her. When I started my sentence with "I don't want to gossip, but . . ." she looked at me and said, "I don't know who you are going to tell me about, but I want to let you know before you gossip about this person, I will go to them and quote what you told me word for word. And I will tell them that you are the one who told me."

I decided to keep it to myself.

Another way to create peace out of conflict is actively to try to bring calm to a turbulent situation. In other words, in many cases God can use you to stand up in the storm of a person's life and say, "Peace, be still."

I know that during one of the most turbulent storms my family has gone through, we had people sit with us and provide that sense of peace. When a young woman who lived with us and called us Mom and Dad died suddenly, our life was a whirlwind of emotions and activity. I remember that in the weeks that followed that tragic loss people would come over to our house. Sometimes they would bring a little plant or a tree and plant it in our yard in honor of Meghan. Other times they'd just sit for an hour or so and listen to me. Occasionally they would just sit next to me and allow me to be silent, but not alone.

In each case, Jesus gave you and I the ability to step into people's lives and say, "Peace, be still."

During my wife's first year at Walla Walla College she and a group of friends would meet on Friday nights to sing and pray and study together at Pastor Doug Ammon's house.

One Friday night everybody showed up and Pastor Doug introduced them to a young woman that hadn't been a part of the group, but was wanting to experience some Jesus time with a group of people her age.

Wendy and the others willingly accepted her into their group. The pastor had an appointment, but just before he left he pulled one of the young men aside and said, "Keep an eye on the new girl, Amy. She's been going through some pretty serious things."

The young man agreed, the pastor left, and the group started singing and worshipping together. It was during prayer time that the young man noticed Amy get up and go into the kitchen. He decided to follow her.

When Amy picked up a kitchen knife, it became obvious to him that she intended to harm herself with it. Grabbing her arm, he tried to get the knife away. That's when it happened.

Suddenly superhuman strength filled her, she spoke in deep guttural voices, and her eyes rolled around in their sockets. It took several of the guys to hold her down. Shocked, the young people decided that it would be good for my wife to sing to Amy. She did, and for the duration of each song it seemed that the girl would calm down.

In between songs the voices would emerge from Amy and announce, "She's mine, she's mine."

When Pastor Doug came home later on that evening he found a living room with all the furniture pushed up against the walls (she was flailing and sometimes tossing the guys into it) and with several frightened but determined young people trying to help.

I've spoken to four of the people who were in that room that night. All four of them told me that when the Pastor walked in, it was as if Jesus had entered the room.

Pastor Doug looked at the situation and said, "Amy, your time of confrontation has not yet come. In the name of Jesus Christ, leave her."

Amy went limp, slept for few minutes, woke up, and had no idea what had happened to her.

Pastor Doug allowed Jesus to provide peace in that situation. He stepped into this girl's life without fear and said, "Peace, be still."

I've thought a lot about what it would mean to be a peacemaker. And as I have, I couldn't help but muse about the people I know in my life that are the opposite of peacemakers. I call them troublemakers. People who are always sticking their sticks in other people's spokes, people who are easily red faced and upset about things, people who seem always to have to express a contrary opinion that rocks the boat and riles things up . . . troublemakers. Do you know anybody like that?

Now, I'm not saying that there isn't a place for differing opinions and debate. We need those things to be able to think and decide and learn.

But I do mean that there are people who are less devil's advocate and more devil, who get some sort of perverse thrill out of making people's lives hard because they are right and everybody else is wrong. Feeling justified in their gossip, they believe it's OK to stir up trouble. People like that are troublemakers, not peacemakers.

It's really easy to tear people down. But how much more peace would it bring to a situation to build somebody up instead?

"Do not let any unwholesome talk come out of your mouths, but only what is helpful for building others up according to their needs" (Eph.. 4:29).

Peacemakers build up—they don't tear down. They make peace by relieving the burden of trouble from people's lives. I run into people all the time who have the spiritual gift of doing exactly that. They are the ones who work behind the scenes, the unsung heroes that make life better.

What can you do to help relieve the stress of everyday life and create peace instead? The people in the parable of the sheep and goats found in Matthew 25 created peace in the lives of the thirsty, the hungry, the naked, the poor, and the imprisoned. Their actions gained heavenly recognition.

Jesus said, "Come unto me, all ye that labour and are heavy laden, and I will give you rest" (Matt. 11:28, KJV). I believe that He has called us to provide a sense of that same kind of rest to those around us. And I believe He wants us to provide peace in the midst of the storm in people's lives. As we become peacemakers, we become more and more of the people that God has called us to be.

"Blessed are the peacemakers, for they shall be called sons of God."

CHAPTER 10

Jesus' Teaching on the Mount: Jesus the Merciful

I found an extreme example of mercy at Mount Pisgah Academy when I was chaplain there. One evening one of our faculty members who didn't have a reputation for being lenient, much less merciful, walked out a door and nearly stumbled over a couple embracing more vigorously than the rules allowed.

When he asked the young couple to stop and head for the dorms, the young man flew off the handle and started arguing with him. The situation heated up until the young man started swearing and cursing, using colorful metaphors to describe the staff member's immediate family.

At faculty meeting that night the teacher reported the incident, and everybody expected that the young man would get kicked out of school. It was just a matter of calling his parents and helping him pack his things in the boys' dorm.

Instead, something else happened.

In tears, the offended faculty member suggested that the school suspend the young man for three days. And since the student was from Florida (the school is in North Carolina), he offered to let the young man meet out the suspension at the staffer's own home. "Maybe if he stays with us," he said, "we can mend the relationship and come out of this thing friends instead of enemies."

The motion passed, and the young man remained with the faculty member for three days. A friendship developed, and the past became the past.

"Blessed are the merciful, for they will be shown mercy" (Matt. 5:7).

Mercy is quite a word, isn't it? It packs meaning and emotion. My online dictionary defines it this way: "1. compassionate or kindly forbearance shown toward an offender, an enemy, or other person in one's power; compassion, pity, or benevolence. 2. the disposition to be compassionate or forbearing. 3. the discretionary power of a judge to pardon someone or to mitigate punishment, especially to send to prison rather than invoke the death penalty. 4. an act of kindness, compassion, or favor. 5. something that gives evidence of divine favor."

Have you ever desired mercy?

When I was a teenager I had a car full of friends who wanted to go cruising on a popular avenue. The problem was that we had a near empty gas tank and a bunch of empty pockets.

One of the girls with us said, "We could sneak on to my parents' property and siphon gas from their station wagon. They sleep really hard. They'll never hear a thing."

We all decided it was worth the risk, so we got a gas can and a hose and parked in the dark at the front of their driveway. The girl and I snuck up the driveway and popped open the gas door. Unscrewing the cap, we stuck the hose in. I sucked on the end of the hose until I got half a mouthful of gasoline and started letting gravity do its work as the five-gallon drum started to fill up.

Suddenly a bright light flashed in our faces as the owner of the house, my family doctor, stood in the driveway next to us.

We were busted. Guilty from the get-go. No explanation other than that we were evil teenagers stealing someone's gas.

He brought us into the house for what I supposed would be either a wait for a police officer or, at the least, a call to my parents and no car for a month.

After we sat down, the owner of the car said, "Hey, Mark, if you would have talked to me I would have given you $20 for gas. You didn't have to steal from me." And then he gave me $20.

The Bible uses the word "mercy" hundreds of times to describe the basic need of every human being. We need mercy.

Those who require mercy find themselves at a decided disadvantage. They must seek help from those able to give that aid, because they cannot supply that assistance themselves.

At one level we see this played out several times while Jesus was on earth. As He walked around He dispensed mercy to those people who found themselves knocked around physically, mentally, and spiritually.

"Leaving that place, Jesus withdrew to the region of Tyre and Sidon. A Canaanite woman from that vicinity came to him, crying out, 'Lord, Son of David, have mercy on me! My daughter is demon-possessed and suffering terribly.' Jesus did not answer a word. So his disciples came to him and urged him, 'Send her away, for she keeps crying out after us.' He answered, 'I was sent only to the lost sheep of Israel.' The woman came and knelt before him. 'Lord, help me!' she said. He replied, 'It is not right to take the children's bread and toss it to the dogs.' 'Yes it is, Lord,' she said. 'Even the dogs eat the crumbs that fall from their master's table.' Then Jesus said to her, 'Woman, you have great faith! Your request is granted.' And her daughter was healed at that moment" (Matt. 15:21-28).

Notice the nature of mercy here. The One who extended mercy didn't have a list of demands for the person receiving it. He just heard the request and then He acted mercifully.

Mercy isn't an exchange of items. It's not a matter of I'll scratch your back if you scratch mine. Instead, mercy is extended as a gift, simply because one person needs it and the other person has the heart to dispense it.

The Bible does a great job of painting the truth about the human condition. We are all in need of mercy. And it isn't something that shows up from time to time—we must have mercy every hour, every day, every moment.

The law is like a mirror for us. As we look into it and discover the real nature of who we are, we see that sin has so tainted our hearts to the point at which we may not realize our condition even if someone were to tell it to us.

We are steeped in pride, greed, and selfishness. It's our nature, something we inherited. All of us always need mercy.

Sometimes realizing the necessity of mercy can be quite a challenge for some people. I mean, we're not that bad, right? I go to church. I pay my taxes. It's not as if I'm like those people walking around out there doing all those terrible things . . .

To some who were confident of their own righteousness and looked down on everybody else, Jesus told a parable: "Two men went up to the temple to pray, one a Pharisee and the other a tax collector. The Pharisee stood by himself and prayed: 'God, I thank you that I am not like other people—robbers, evildoers, adulterers—or even like this tax collector. I fast twice a week and give a tenth of all I get.' But the tax collector stood at a distance. He would not even look up to heaven, but beat his breast and said, 'God, have mercy on me, a sinner.' I tell you that this man, rather than the other, went home justified before God. For all those who exalt themselves will be humbled, and those who humble themselves will be exalted" (Luke 18:9-14).

You see, the beauty of our God of mercy is that in each and every case, anyone who has ever asked God for mercy, gets it. Period. It's just that some people are so steeped in pride they don't realize they need it.

Never did Jesus, when He encountered someone in need of mercy, look at them and then blow them off. There has never been a person on earth who has cried out for mercy that God hasn't granted it to.

From the very beginning we find God associated with the idea of mercy. In fact, as indicated by how the earthly sanctuary was laid out, the closer you got to God the closer you got to mercy.

What was it that sat atop the ark of the covenant where God resided? Yes, the mercy seat—the place that one would look to to receive mercy.

And as we consider the sanctuary in heaven, as broken and beat up by sin as we all are, the Bible says that we may still approach the throne of grace with boldness. Why? Because sitting on that mercy seat is the One who is merciful. We go there not to be condemned, but to receive the mercy and grace that is the very nature of our God.

Now remember, we didn't earn mercy because of something we did. God gives it because we needed it—*even before we wanted it.*

"And you were dead in your trespasses and sins, in which you formerly walked according to the course of this world, according to the prince of the power of the air, of the spirit that is now working in the sons of disobedience. Among them we too all formerly lived in the lusts of our flesh, indulging the desires of the flesh and of the mind, and were by nature children of wrath, even as the rest. But God, being rich in mercy, because of His great love with which He loved us, even when we were dead in our transgressions, made us alive together with Christ (by grace you have been saved), and raised us up with Him, and seated us with Him in the heavenly places, in Christ Jesus, so that in the ages to come He might show the surpassing riches of His grace in kindness toward us in Christ Jesus. For by grace you have been saved through faith; and that not of yourselves, it is the gift of God" (Eph. 2:1-8, NASB).

In a very real sense God extended His mercy to me, a sinner, even before I knew I must have it. The mercy I received from Him came while I was yet His enemy.

Revelation 13:8 is so awe-inspiring we just have to ponder it here. "All inhabitants of the earth will worship the beast—all whose names have not been written in the Lamb's book of life, the Lamb who was slain from the creation of the world."

The Lamb had been slain from the creation of the world. The inference here is that the mercy extended to us at the cross didn't just start there at Calvary. God's mercy toward His children began even before our creation. The Source of mercy gave us mercy before we even asked for it.

"I thank Christ Jesus our Lord, who has strengthened me, because He considered me faithful, putting me into service, even though I was formerly a blasphemer and a persecutor and a violent aggressor. Yet I was shown mercy because I acted ignorantly in unbelief; and the grace of our Lord was more than abundant, with the faith and love which are found in Christ

Jesus. It is a trustworthy statement, deserving full acceptance, that Christ Jesus came into the world to save sinners, among whom I am foremost of all. Yet for this reason I found mercy, so that in me as the foremost, Jesus Christ might demonstrate His perfect patience as an example for those who would believe in Him for eternal life" (1 Tim. 1:12-16, NASB).

Notice that Paul received mercy while he was steeped in sin. Not afterward. In fact, God's mercy actually knocked him off of a horse to get his attention!

God extends His mercy to you right now. At this very moment He gives you the gift of salvation. Mercy is yours if you want it. Our wonderful God meets every genuine cry for spiritual mercy with kindness and compassion. No application is denied . . . almost.

I say almost because just as salvation is God's gift to every human being that has ever drawn breath, not all will experience that salvation. Sadly, some will reject that divine gift.

And even though God offers mercy to every human being, not every human being will accept it.

"Therefore, the kingdom of heaven is like a king who wanted to settle accounts with his servants. As he began the settlement, a man who owed him ten thousand bags of gold was brought to him. Since he was not able to pay, the master ordered that he and his wife and his children and all that he had be sold to repay the debt. At this the servant fell on his knees before him. 'Be patient with me,' he begged, 'and I will pay back everything.' The servant's master took pity on him, canceled the debt and let him go. But when that servant went out, he found one of his fellow servants who owed him a hundred silver coins. He grabbed him and began to choke him. 'Pay back what you owe me!' he demanded. His fellow servant fell to his knees and begged him, 'Be patient with me, and I will pay you back.' But he refused. Instead, he went off and had the man thrown into prison until he could pay the debt. When the other servants saw what had happened, they were outraged and went and told their master everything that had happened. Then the master called the servant in. 'You wicked servant,' he said, 'I canceled all that debt of yours because you begged me to. Shouldn't you have had mercy on your fellow servant just as I had on you?' In anger his master turned him over to the jailers to be tortured, until he should pay back all he owed. This is how my heavenly Father will treat each of you unless you forgive your brother from your heart" (Matt. 18:23-35).

Receiving mercy has a responsibility that comes with it . . . and that responsibility is that we must extend mercy to one another. The big beef that Jesus had with the religious leadership of His day was just that.

"Woe to you, scribes and Pharisees, hypocrites! For you tithe mint and dill and cummin, and have neglected the weightier provisions of the law: justice and mercy and faithfulness; but these are the things you should have done without neglecting the others" (Matt. 23:23, NASB).

Jesus reiterated this teaching in Luke 10 in the parable of the good Samaritan. A religion scholar asked Him what he needed to do to gain eternal life. At the end of the story Jesus asked who the good neighbor was, and the man answered, " 'The one who showed mercy toward him.' Then Jesus said to him, 'Go and do the same' " (Luke 10:37, NASB).

Why? Because God has shown mercy toward you.

Who are we to hold a grudge? Who are we to put ourselves in the place of God and then act the opposite of Him?

"For judgment will be merciless to one who has shown no mercy; mercy triumphs over judgment" (James 2:13, NASB). We are called to be extenders of mercy because we have been given that very gift.

Take a moment to think about those to whom you have not extended the hand of mercy to in your life. Who is it that you are holding that grudge toward?

"But when the kindness of God our Savior and His love for mankind appeared, He saved us, not on the basis of deeds which we have done in righteousness, but according to His mercy, by the washing of regeneration and renewing by the Holy Spirit, whom He poured out upon us richly through Jesus Christ our Savior" (Titus 3:4-6, NASB).

CHAPTER 11

Jesus' Teaching on the Mount: Jesus Wants Salt

Jesus said in Matthew 5:13: "You are the salt of the earth. But if the salt loses its saltiness, how can it be made salty again? It is no longer good for anything, except to be thrown out and trampled underfoot."

Notice that He didn't say, "You ought to be the salt of the earth" or "You should think about being the salt of the earth," but rather, "You *are* the salt of the earth." Let's consider the metaphor of salt here for a second.

One time when preaching about this topic in my local church I had a volunteer come up front and I gave them a spoonful of plain tofu. Then I asked the person about its taste. The person replied that it was bland and tasteless.

Then I took another spoonful of tofu and dumped a huge pile of salt on it. The person made faces and nearly spit it out on my pulpit. That much salt on anything, he said, ruined the taste.

In order for salt to do its job properly, it needs to be sprinkled just right and mixed through the food to give it just the proper flavor.

When I used to speak for *It Is Written*'s Partnership meetings I always looked forward to the food that the hotels would provide for us. I love to eat, so for me all that free food was quite a treat.

One weekend in San Diego the hotel staff served postchurch lunch in a huge ballroom. I was sitting at a table with Shawn and Jeanie Boonstra, and we were having a marvelous time talking, laughing, and sharing our stories of faith together. Finally the main course came out. Amongst the other things on the plate was a piece of pie-shaped lukewarm tofu that had been rolled in cornflakes and placed on the plate. It wasn't that it tasted bad—rather that it had no taste at all. Asking for a bowl of tartar sauce, I slathered it on my tofu. That made it even worse. I could have just eaten the tartar sauce and had the same taste in my mouth.

As Shawn and I walked around the room and greeted people during lunch, we noticed that nobody ate their tofu pie.

"Be wise in the way you act toward outsiders; make the most of every opportunity. Let your conversation be always full of grace, seasoned with salt, so that you may know how to answer everyone" (Col. 4:5, 6).

Paul seems to be calling for a balanced speech toward those who do not know the gospel, one salted with captivating intrigue and seasoned with grace.

Have you ever seen anybody use the gospel as a hammer?

In a parable of a vacuum cleaner salesmen written by John Duckworth, a young man trying to sell his first vacuum cleaner sets up a soapbox on a sidewalk and yells at the people walking by.

"You pigs!" he proclaims, "You who have filthy and dirty floors! Repent of your filthy floor ways and buy a vacuum cleaner!"

After shouting at people about their need for a vacuum cleaner for most of the day, the man steps down and says, "H'mmm. They must have all been convicted of their filth and gone home to get their money to buy a vacuum from me."

Of course the people never come back, and the man goes home discouraged.

I can't tell you how many people I've talked to that want nothing to do with the church, because they have felt beat up by the gospel of too much salt. Any time we use the gospel of Jesus Christ to berate or to belittle or to guilt-trip people into correct behavior, we are making a mistake. Remember, too much salt in one's diet can raise your blood pressure and endanger your health.

Paul says that our conversations should be full of grace and only seasoned with salt. Any time we give people a big spoonful of salt because we are convinced that that's what they need, we have done damage to the gospel and misrepresented God.

Jesus says it in another way in Mark 9:50: "Salt is good, but if it loses its saltiness, how can you make it salty again? Have salt in yourselves, and be at peace with each other." It seems that here in the book of Mark, Jesus is giving us a clear call not to be plain old tofu Christians.

The adjective here in the Greek that would be a clear synonym to the phrase "losing its saltiness" is the word "insipid." My computer dictionary says: "Insipid: *adjective* 1. without distinctive, interesting, or stimulating qualities; vapid. 2. without sufficient taste to be pleasing, as food or drink; bland."

On the other side of the danger of being too salty is the warning for us not to be the opposite of that. It seems that every road has a rut on either side of it that we can get stuck in.

The rut on the opposite side of assaulting people with the gospel and driving them away with too much salt is being such a bland tofu believer that the appeal of a life in Jesus never shines through our lives.

I've had lots of people tell me that they are going to be silent witnesses for the gospel. They will just let their life speak for itself. So they go to work, mow their lawn, do their grocery shopping, go on vacation, come to church, sit on a pew, get a blessing . . . but rarely lift a finger to give a blessing.

They sit but they don't participate. They believe . . . kind of . . . but not enough to lead them into any kind of risk for the gospel. Their fear of salt has turned them into tofu Christians.

Jesus declared, "Salt is good, but if it loses its saltiness, how can it be made salty again? It is fit neither for the soil nor for the manure pile; it is thrown out" (Luke 14:34, 35).

Can you imagine being so worthless that we aren't even deserving of the manure pile? To lose our saltiness, to lose our desire to make a difference in this world, to become tofu Christians, is to make the gospel ineffective in the world around us, and I would dare say, maybe even make the gospel worthless to ourselves.

Tofu Christians play church until it becomes little more than a routine. We come to church like we take our medicine—we do it because it's good for us. That's what happens when we lose our saltiness.

Did you know that God has considered salt an important metaphor for the believer's life from the very beginning? That each and every sacrifice brought to the sanctuary and placed on the altar, whether it was an animal sacrifice or a grain sacrifice, had to be mixed with salt before being placed on the altar? It was called the covenant of salt. You can find the salt of sacrifices in Numbers 18:19 and Leviticus 2:13.

Whether it was a sin offering or a thank offering, whatever you brought to the Lord as a sacrifice, it was always to be rubbed down with salt before being deposited on the altar.

"Therefore, I urge you, brothers and sisters, in view of God's mercy, to offer your bodies as a living sacrifice, holy and pleasing to God—this is your true and proper worship" (Rom. 12:1).

We are to present our bodies—those living sacrifices—before the Lord with the salt of the gospel. Salt preserves, salt seasons, salt cures.

Jesus tells us that we, as Christians, are to be salt in the world. We are to be a seasoning, a preservative, and a cure in a world full of sin and hatred toward God and the things of God.

Salt melts ice. The right amount of salt, seasoned in our lives, can thaw the ice about God that has formed in the heart of a neighbor. Many times people form opinions about God because of how the "frozen chosen" have presented Him. The right amount of salt in a relationship with that person can really thaw the ice.

One of the most evident salty experiences I've had is when I cry. Have you ever had a tear roll down your face and end up in your mouth? What does it taste like? Salt.

When you cry, your tears taste salty. And when you sit with someone going through a storm in their life and cry with them, you are being the salt of the earth. That salt is the sharing of pain and the healing of a wound.

It's hard to be the salt of the earth if we live in such a way that we don't even notice the people around us. If we fall into a tofu life, bland and without meaning, we cannot be the salt of the earth. And if that's what our church becomes, than we are not even fit for the dung heap.

I would say, go ahead and eat as much tofu as you want—it's good for you. But don't become a tofu Christian. You are the salt of the earth. Act like it.

CHAPTER 12

Blessed are the pure in heart, for they shall see God" (Matt. 5:8, NKJV). The word "blessed" and the word "happy" are the same word in the original language of the New Testament. So read a different way, it says that those who have pure hearts are happy people, and more than that, they will see God.

But what does it mean to be "pure in heart"? It has a few different levels to it.

First and foremost, on a very surface level, a person who is pure in heart is someone who practices telling the truth. To put it another way, they aren't liars.

Do you remember the first time you ever told a lie? When I was 3 years old my family lived in Pasadena, California. One day I was out in the front yard playing while my dad worked on the car. Hearing what I thought was the familiar sound of the ice-cream truck coming down the street, I got so excited that I decided to hunt it down and get some ice cream. Before long, however, I was lost, finding myself in a little café. A police officer sat at the counter. I asked him if he had seen the ice cream truck. He flipped a nickel on the counter, and the man behind the counter gave me an ice-cream cone. I left and somehow found my way home.

As I came up the driveway, my dad slid out from under the car and asked, "Where did you get that ice cream?" Even at 3 years old, I knew that I'd get a spanking if I told him what had happened. So I lied and said that the neighbor woman had given it to me.

Immediately I ran into the house, dropped my ice cream, and started crying. Then I flew into my mother's arms and told her about my lie.

It seems that from the beginning we somehow start out with hearts that need to go through some sort of purification process. We aren't born with pure hearts. Our tendency from a pretty young age is to lie to get out of difficult situations.

Once upon a time a little boy had a hard time telling the truth. His mother struggled with the child's lies, so she finally said to him, "Did you know that every time you lie, a little light goes off on your forehead, and that's how I always find out?"

The next day the little boy rushed into the kitchen with his hand over his forehead. "Mom! The dog just broke your favorite lamp!"

The first character trait that God offers people who strive after a pure heart is basic verbal honesty, no matter the consequence. And the Bible elaborates on this throughout its pages.

In fact, several verses down from this beatitude, Jesus says that when someone asks you to make a commitment, let your "yes" mean "yes" and your "no" mean "no." Just leave it at that. Don't go swearing on a stack of Bibles, or crossing your heart and hoping to die.

If you have a pure heart, eventually people will view you as a person of your word. And because you are pure in heart, people will know that what you say never intentionally misleads. You will be someone who tells the truth.

But being pure in heart goes beyond just telling the truth. When the Bible speaks about a person's heart, it's not talking about the organ that's beating in our chests. It has in mind our inner recesses, the place where we feel deeply, where we make secret decisions. The Bible calls our heart the site where we mix our rational and our emotional lives. Our heart is what we are, who we are, when all of the pretenses and masks are stripped away. In essence, our heart is our soul, uncovered.

Consequently, being pure in heart means that a godly integrity fills the deepest recesses of our lives. My word processor offers these synonyms for the word "integrity": credibility, fidelity, honor, nobility, principle, character, decency, dignity, guiltlessness.

People who live lives of integrity (pure in heart) do so with honesty, not only in word, but also in action. The pure in heart have pure motives. They do everything for the right reasons. No hidden agenda, no manipulation to get their way or to gain personal satisfaction. Pure in heart people live their lives—even their secret lives—with sincere motives.

When I was about 11 years old my mom wanted me to learn what it was like to do nice things just for the satisfaction of doing them. In my neighborhood lived an 87-year-old woman. She had a hard time getting around and wasn't able to mow her grass very well anymore. So my mom asked me if I wanted to do it.

"Sure," I said. "How much will I get paid?"

"Nothing. I want you to do it just to be nice."

I'd never heard of anything so ludicrous in my life. *Thanks, Mom, but I'll pass on the freebee,* I thought to myself.

"OK," my mother said, "how about if you go mow her lawn for free and I increase your allowance by $10 per week?"

"Deal."

So I went down to Anna's house and mowed her lawn once a week. The whole time she would follow me around and show me the places I missed. She would also make me stop the lawn mower, take a shovel, and rid her lawn of the land mines the neighbor's dogs would leave on a regular basis.

One day, after I finished mowing her lawn, Anna came out to send me off and said, "You are such a nice boy. I don't think I've ever met a young man who would sacrifice an afternoon just to mow an old lady's lawn and not get paid for it."

Without thinking, I responded, "I wouldn't do this for free. My mom is paying me or I wouldn't even think of doing this."

As she turned and walked back into the house, her face dropped. Her disappointment came from a sense that what I was doing didn't have pure motives at all. In fact, my motives were tainted to the point that if my mother hadn't increased my allowance, I wouldn't have ventured near Anna's yard at all.

One of the things that just seems to come along with being a human being is that we all suffer from questionable motives—at least from time to time. Sometimes that can be benign, but often it can be disastrous. How many times have we all seen people get married for reasons that maybe weren't so pure? How many guys have asked girls out on dates with some sort of hidden agenda? How many business transactions have little to no honesty on the part of one or both of the participants?

God offers people who want to be pure in heart a life of integrity. He seeks to give us a life that will do the right things for the right reasons.

Some of our hearts are so tainted that it has affected our religion. When we ask people why they are Christians, their answer is often "So I can go to heaven!"

Interesting motive. At least they're honest. But, when you think about it, that would be like answering your wife with "I got married to you so I could have a legal physical intimacy." How romantic.

God wants to give us pure motives, even when it comes to the reasons that we follow Him. He seeks for us to be in a relationship with Him so that we can fall in love with and trust Him as it's our privilege to do so.

And those motives go beyond the surface actions that other people can observe in our lives. The Lord desires to reach deeply into our secret life—the times that we live out our morality when we are by ourselves and nobody is looking.

Men, wouldn't you love to have a pure heart and pure motives in your relationships with other women? When you are alone on a trip in a hotel room and you get your choice of movies, could He give you a heart that would reject the chance to order a movie that strips the dignity away from women? God wants to do that.

Often we find ourselves with our backs up against the wall in life and struggle to resist lashing out to save ourselves or to get what we want. Wouldn't it be nice, then, to put others ahead of ourselves and consider ourselves as servants?

Or when tempted to paint the truth with a little lie to make ourselves look better, wouldn't it be nice to know that Jesus is our All in All and be content with that and not have to worry about what other people think about us?

The third thing that God offers to a person who desires to have a pure heart is ironical in a way. The word Jesus used that we translate as "pure" in English is the same one that the Bible employs elsewhere to describe food. The Bible designated foods as fit or unfit to eat by the terms "clean" or "unclean."

The word translated as "clean" in regard to food is the same one that Jesus applies to a human heart. In other words, the phrase could say, "Blessed are people with a clean heart, for they shall see God."

It reflects on David's post-Bathsheba Psalm 51 as he begs God to give him a clean heart with pure motives. Not a one of us hasn't let our passion for any number of things taint our pure heart.

Having a clean heart means that you have a heart free of the guilt usually associated with sinning. A clean heart and a clear conscience are virtually the same thing.

What's the worst thing you've ever done? What is that one habit or practice in your life that you just can't seem to shake? What are the parts of your secret life that nobody else knows about, ones that weigh on your heart and make it anything but clean?

Whatever they might be, wherever they came from, God wants to take them from you and leave you with the clean, pure heart that we all want so badly inside. And although it may be a gradual process, God's forgiveness releases a cleansing flood of purity and freedom that will set your heart on a journey that will lead to that life of integrity you've always wanted to have. Guilt-free hearts are pure hearts.

The reason a person with a pure heart can see God is because they can now understand the heart of God Himself. Such individuals recognize that He is integrity and truth personified. His cleansing forgiveness provides a solution for a guilt-free, clean heart that no earthly craving can satisfy.

"Blessed are the pure in heart, for they shall see God." The Bible teaches us that if we want a pure heart, it's ours for the asking. Scripture promises that if we decide to walk with God, He will make us into a new creation, one with a pure heart—a heart after God.

CHAPTER 13

Jesus in Jericho

Jericho was one of those places that seemed to have it all. It had a rich history that archaeologists say makes it one of the oldest inhabited cities in the world. The city even had ties to Cleopatra and Mark Antony until they leased it out to King Herod, who kept a winter palace there. In fact, all of the surrounding aristocracy considered Jericho to be their personal resort town . . . a lifestyles of the rich and famous kind of town during certain seasons.

But Jericho was also a place of commerce. It was a major stop on the way to Jerusalem. The story of the good Samaritan took place on that road.

There had even been some recent intrigue in Jericho that happened during a party that Herod the Great's mother-in-law, Alexandra, had thrown. During it some of Herod's servants and friends invited her son Aristobulus to go swimming with them. Pretending to play around, they held his head underwater until he drowned. It was such big news that a historian named Josephus wrote about it almost 70 years after it happened.

Jericho was kind of like the Peyton Place of the cities of Jesus' time. Lots of scuttlebutt circulated through it. The Jericho *Inquirer* was the best-selling paper at the grocery store. Inquiring minds wanted to know even then!

It was also a beautiful city. In the book *The Desire of Ages* Ellen White tells us that it was filled with gardens and palm trees and springs. Archeology reveals to us that its inhabitants channeled those springs into aqueducts to water the outlying areas and gardens. Jericho was quite the happening place.

So you can imagine the stir that happened there when news started spreading that Jesus was coming to town. He was making his final journey to Jerusalem and word got out that He would pass through the city.

Can you imagine the curious people, the sick people, the religious people who all wanted to maybe just catch a glimpse of the famous Rabbi who had had a following like nobody they'd ever seen?

Jesus had become quite the curiosity by the end of His ministry. He'd been through many of the minor towns outside of Jerusalem, preaching and healing. The religious establishment was certainly aware of Him, even suspicious of this Teacher who claimed to have the authority to forgive sins. The people in Judea and its surrounding areas had heard Him say that "the kingdom of God is at hand!" Did it mean that He would free Israel once and for all from the Romans? And now He and the multitude that followed Him were coming into Jericho.

Just on the outskirts of Jericho a blind man named Bartimaeus heard a ruckus. He could tell from the noise and excited speech of the people around him that something exciting was happening. "What's going on?" he asked.

"Jesus of Nazareth is entering Jericho," people told him. "Can you believe it?"

Even the blind beggar had heard that Jesus was the Great Physician, the Great Healer. Word had reached him how Jesus had spit on the eyes of a blind man to restore his sight. Bartimaeus couldn't contain himself anymore. Here was his chance finally to see!

"Jesus! Son of David! Have mercy on me!" It seemed the louder he yelled, the noisier the crowd got.

"JESUS! SON OF DAVID! HAVE MERCY ON ME!"

The blind man could feel a shift in the crowd and then a hush as each person on the outskirts of Jericho, all those curious people who wanted to get a glimpse of Jesus, listened and watched. They wanted to see something special—didn't want to miss a thing.

The blind man heard the Savior's voice. "What do you want Me to do for you?"

It must be Jesus—it had to be.

The request was simple. The man didn't need to beat around the bush. "Lord, I want to see!"

Jesus smiled and said, "Your faith has healed you. Go ahead, see."

Immediately a flood of colors passed through the man's corneas and then through his pupils. Light raced through to his retinas and the rods and cones produced electrical impulses that zipped up his optic nerve to his brain, giving him his first blast of sight!

And the first thing the man ever saw was Jesus of Nazareth, the one who healed him.

Astonished, the crowd started calling out praises to God. Gasps of amazement as well as scoff from the outskirts of the mob of people began to gain momentum as Jesus started to enter the city. More and more clustered around Him as He made His way through Jericho. It was noisy and exciting, but it was getting difficult to negotiate the streets with all the vendors selling their wares and all of the sick and afflicted trying to get their chance for healing.

The crowd pressed on all sides. Jesus' disciples had formed a circle around Him, attempting to guard Him from the people, especially those kinds considered "unworthy" of His presence.

As the crowd moved along at a reasonable pace, all of a sudden Jesus paused under a tree . . . maybe for some shade on the too-hot day.

But Jesus wasn't stopping for shade, because when He halted, He looked up. And when Jesus looked up, so did everybody else.

A man sat in the tree. Not something you'd see every day. It seemed that he was almost hiding up there, trying not to be noticed, maybe sneaking a peek at what all the excitement was about.

Zacchaeus was a wee little man. But that's not all that he was. The Bible tells us that he was a "chief tax collector." Rome's method of collecting taxes was to employ as tax collectors locals that knew who had money and where they kept it. The occupation government divided a province into tax districts. People would bid for the contract of collecting taxes in a district. The bid was the money they promised to pay Rome. Whatever they collected over that amount was theirs to keep. The chief tax collector (such as Zacchaeus) owned the contract for his region. And remember, Jericho was a wealthy place. Zacchaeus had won the bid to supply taxes for Rome. Then he would employ others to collect taxes in the various villages.

Rome collected three principal kinds of taxes: (1) a land tax, (2) a head tax, and (3) a customs tax of 2 to 5 percent of the value of goods transported through a district. Zacchaeus had charge of all the tax collectors who would impose the Roman tax, plus collect a profit for Zacchaeus, and then finally take a little for themselves.

People hated tax collectors, but even more, they hated the chief tax collector, because he was the guy that negotiated the bid with the Romans in the first place! He was also the one with the big house in town that was paid for with their hard-earned money.

Yes, Zacchaeus was a wee little man, but he was also a powerful, wealthy, unpopular one . . . in a tree.

Why was he in a tree? Seems like a strange place for a grown man to be hanging out. Well, weeks, maybe months before Jesus' arrival in Jericho, Zacchaeus had heard something strange. A colleague of his had had an encounter with Jesus. His name was Levi Matthew . . . a man who had a lot in common with Zacchaeus. What Jesus said and taught had so changed Levi Matthew that he had actually given it all up, dropped everything, handed over his bid to another tax collector, and followed the Rabbi.

Rumor claimed that Levi Matthew was a converted man with a new heart and a new lease on life!

Zacchaeus had long had a hole in his heart. He knew that he had conducted business in dishonest ways and realized that he had increased the hardship of the people in Jericho and in its surrounding villages. And he wondered if there was any hope for a man like him. *Could God love even me?* he wondered. *I may be a part of the chosen people, but I don't feel very chosen.*

Not only had he heard about Levi Matthew, but word had it that Jesus even kind of liked tax collectors. Maybe, just maybe, if he could just get close enough to Jesus, then perhaps he could find the acceptance and the love that he had heard so much about. Maybe he could find at least one person who wasn't a tax collector that would be his friend . . . maybe.

When he learned that Jesus had entered the city, Zacchaeus ran to the outskirts of the crowd to catch a glimpse of the good Rabbi. But the thick wall of people was too much for him to penetrate.

Not only was the unintentional wall too big for Zacchaeus, but the intentional one that formed as people started to realize that it was Zacchaeus who was trying to get to Jesus surpassed unfriendly and got downright violent. An accidental elbow to the forehead and a heel to the foot of the height-impaired tax collector drove him away from the crowd, dejected and rejected. Nobody wanted him there. Perhaps not even Jesus.

But Zacchaeus deserved it, and he knew it. Nobody in this town was going to do him any favors. The official had made their lives miserable, and now it was their turn to get him back.

With a sigh he looked up the street. That's when he saw it—the tree in the middle of the street that Jesus was bound to walk down. What if he were to get up in that tree without anyone noticing . . . then he might at least catch a glimpse of the Rabbi. Perhaps he could see a miracle or hear the Master speak a word of acceptance to someone like him. Maybe that would be enough.

Making an instant decision, he ran ahead of the crowd and climbed the tree as fast as he could. Hiding in the branches, he hoped that nobody would see him. I mean, how embarrassing for a man to be hiding in a tree. And if they did spot him, surely the people would start telling Jesus what a crook he was.

The crowd approached, and Jesus paused—and looked up.

Oh, no. I think He sees me. Oh, no.

"Zacchaeus. Come down."

This can't be good. I am so busted. Should I say no? But wait, He knows my name! The Rabbi knows my name!

It was then that Zacchaeus realized that not only did Jesus know his name but also his desire to be right with God again. Zacchaeus the chief tax collector came down out of the tree . . . right in front of Jesus.

"Zacchaeus, I'm going to stay at your house today."

The church people and the townspeople surrounding Jesus were indignant. Does the Rabbi know who this guy is? Does He know that this wee little man is a sinner? A tax collector? A collaborator with the hated Romans?

Church people seem to be the most judgmental people in the world, don't they? Why is that? I mean, you'd think that when Jesus, the leader of all Christians, tells His followers, "Don't judge, lest ye be judged," they'd listen and obey.

Before Jesus could even answer his critics, Zacchaues spoke up, "Lord Jesus, I'm going to give half of everything I have to the poor. And if I've cheated anyone out of anything, I'll pay them back times four." In other words, "I've not been a good man. But today I'm confessing my sins and want to make things right with the people around me. I'm a changed man."

Jesus has that kind of effect on people, doesn't He? When people meet Him—really meet Him—it changes everything.

The Savior's response to Zacchaeus' pronouncement flabbergasted the crowd, but especially the church people. "Today salvation has come to this house, because this man, too, is a son of Abraham. For the Son of Man came to seek and to save what was lost" (Luke 19:9, 10).

Who are you in this story? Are you the blind man in need of Jesus' healing touch? Do you find yourself yelling, "Jesus, son of David, have mercy on me"?

Are you a follower of Jesus ridiculing the person trying to get His attention? Have you become so judgmental and so critical of others that you've actually become an obstacle to Jesus rather than an avenue for people to find the Savior?

Are you Zacchaeus, a person who has been leading a life that would make your mother and maybe even your God blush? Are you someone who needs to make things right with those around you? Are you a person just longing to get a glimpse of Jesus?

Or might you be one of the people surrounding Jesus, guarding and protecting Him from those who might not be worthy to get close to Him? Have you become a guardian of the church, making sure that things are done just so, not letting anything or anyone approach Jesus unless they do it in the proper way? Jesus doesn't need bodyguards . . . and neither does His church.

Or are you Jesus (in this story), someone who's life is so in tune with the Spirit of God that you stop in the middle of your day to notice anyone hurting and in need of salvation? Maybe even somebody that everyone else thinks is despicable.

Are you like Jesus in this story, someone who has decided to be an includer and not an excluder? Are you willing to risk your reputation to go into the house of a sinner, just for the chance to share the good news of the gospel? Becoming all things to all people that you might save one?

You know, sometimes we get so busy in our lives that we don't even notice those who need our healing touch. We get so zealous about what we believe that we unthinkingly put other church members who act out of line (with what we consider proper) on our Zacchaeus list.

A lot of people followed Jesus that day. I don't want to be like the rest of the crowd.

I want to be like Jesus.

CHAPTER 14

Jesus the Confessor

"Whoever conceals their sins does not prosper, but the one who confesses and renounces them finds mercy" (Prov. 28:13).

King David had it all. Having slain the champion Goliath and outlasted and outfoxed King Saul, he was now the ruler of a country that could hold its own, standing between the major powers of the ancient Near East. David had built up the kingdom's military and treasury. And best of all, he led his country in worship and devotion to the God of Abraham, Isaac, and Jacob. Israel was a country on the right track.

As the Bible tells the story, it was springtime, the period of the year when armies went to war to defend or expand the borders of their country. For some reason this time King David sent his forces off to fight while he stayed behind.

One evening he couldn't sleep. Perhaps it was just too hot. Maybe he worried about his army and their success. Who knows, but at some point in the evening he found himself pacing on his balcony.

And that is when he saw her. Because people had no indoor plumbing, they had to bathe where they could. In Bathsheba's case that place was on her rooftop, just below the king's balcony.

The sight of her was too much for his vivid imagination. Now, at the moment of temptation, David had a choice. He could have turned his head and fled from temptation or summoned one of his many wives or concubines. Perhaps he could have taken a cold bath himself.

Instead he summoned the married woman into his chambers, and, well, the rest is history.

When he found out that she had conceived while her husband was off fighting for the kingdom, David did his best to cover up his sin, to keep his wrongdoing in the dark.

Ordering Bathsheba's husband home on a furlough, he invited him to go home to be with his wife. But the loyal soldier, a man named Uriah, refused to have that pleasure if his fellow soldiers were out at battle. He was a loyal marine.

So David went to plan B. He invited Uriah over for a meal and saw to it that the soldier had more than enough wine to drink. The king knew that alcohol lowers one's inhibitions and compromises one's values. When Uriah was good and drunk, David sent him home again to be with his wife.

Still, even while inebriated, the man did not visit his wife.

David felt like the only thing he had left to do was to kill Uriah and marry the man's wife to cover his sin. So he did. He arranged for Uriah to die in battle and took Bathsheba as his newest wife.

David must have felt a real sense of relief as he finally was able to sweep his sin into the dark. He would never get caught for what he did.

If that were where the story ended, it would be horribly depressing, wouldn't it? But we don't serve a God of darkness—we serve one of light.

"This is the message we have heard from him and declare to you: God is light; in him there is no darkness at all" (1 John 1:5).

"You, Lord, keep my lamp burning; my God turns my darkness into light" (Ps. 18:28).

"For God, who said, 'Let light shine out of darkness,' made his light shine in our hearts to give us the light of the knowledge of God's glory displayed in the face of Christ" (2 Cor. 4:6).

God doesn't want us to push anything into the darkness. He seeks to bring things out into the light so that we can have the choice to deal with our darkness.

Therefore, the Lord sends the prophet Nathan to the king to allow David to deal with the things he intended to keep hidden. No more secrets.

Nathan comes to the king and judge of Israel with a perplexing problem. He appeals to the monarch's wisdom to solve a kingdom conflict.

The prophet tells him of a rich man in Israel who has thousands of sheep and a vast amount of land. On the edge of his property lives a very poor man who has a wife and kids and one little lamb that is the family pet. They've trained it and call it by name. The lamb even curls up and sleeps at the end of its master's bed. It's a part of the family.

One day the rich man has a party and decides to have lamb chops as the main course of the banquet. But instead of slaughtering one of his many lambs, he sends some thugs to take the little pet lamb of his poor neighbor and slaughter it for the party.

When David hears this story, he gets angry. Smoke starts to pour out of his ears as he stands and yells, "The man who did this shall surely die!"

Nathan looks directly at King David and points a boney finger right at him. "You, sir, are that man."

Blam—light now floods David's darkness.

Have you ever spent time in a very dark room and then had somebody suddenly turn the lights on? It doesn't feel very good at first, does it? It kind of stings. You want the culprit to turn the light back off to relieve the shooting pain in your eyes.

Light flooding darkness doesn't always feel good, but anytime the light of God exposes our darkness it is always a good thing.

King David had a choice. Continuing to push his sin deeper into the dark, he could have killed Nathan and buried his secret with him. But, as grievous as David's sin was, he knew that hiding things was ultimately a soul-crushing thing to do. Later in his life David wrote from experience: "Blessed is the one whose transgressions are forgiven, whose sins are covered. Blessed is the one whose sin the Lord does not count against them and in whose spirit is no deceit. When I kept silent, my bones wasted away through my groaning all day long. For day and night your hand was heavy on me; my strength was sapped as in the heat of summer. Then I acknowledged my sin to you and did not cover up my iniquity. I said, 'I will confess my transgressions to the Lord.' And you forgave the guilt of my sin" (Ps. 32:1-5).

God does not call us into darkness but into the light. Light exposes. Light illuminates. Light doesn't leave anything hidden. And light can hurt.

We can read David's confession in Psalm 51: "Create in me a clean heart, O God, and renew a steadfast spirit within me. Do not cast me away from your presence" (verses 10, 11). "Cleanse me with hyssop, and I will be clean" (verse 7).

When Nathan illuminated David's darkness with light, it stung. The pain must have been unreal. But David chose to allow the light to do its work, and he confessed.

When we confess, we are actually deciding to bring something out of the darkness into the light for people to see. Confession is a powerful thing for things involving both the good and the bad.

Do you remember the first time you ever confessed your love to someone that stole your heart? I still have memories of a couple occasions when as a teenager I had to work up the nerve to confess my love for a girl. It was quite a risk. But eventually I couldn't hold it in the dark any longer, I had to bring it out into the light and say it . . . I love you! And then I had to wait for the response. Most of the time the response was "Really? Wow! Uh, thank you, I guess."

We confess our love for one another because we just can't keep something that cool in the dark. It's not healthy to hold it in! If we did, we could explode!

Whoever said that "confession is good for the soul" knew what they were talking about.

The more secrets we have, the more we keep them in the dark, the more power those things not confessed will have over our lives.

The power of darkness is that of fear. What if someone finds out our secret? What will they think of us? I'd better keep it in the dark to protect myself and hope that nobody ever finds out.

But once the light of truth shines on what we have been hiding in the dark, we don't have to be afraid of people finding out our dirty little secrets anymore.

Victims of abuse will tell you that as long as they kept their secret, it held them captive, but once they told somebody about what had happened to them they experienced a release of sorts. Once they went through the pain of letting light hit that dark part of their lives they discovered a kind of freedom from the darkness that they never could have if they would have continued to suppress their secret.

Confession is good for the soul. I think that's why David wrote the psalms. Again and again he confesses his feelings for God. But secreting things in the dark can turn you into a person that you don't want to be.

My experience has been that the most religiously outspoken people, those who judge others and are vocal about how others do and don't do things, usually have something to hide. Highly critical individuals are usually those who have something that they are desperately afraid of letting out into the light.

Such is often the case with politicians that rail on social issues. Again and again we see those who try to legislate sexual behavior fall by the wayside of sexual deviancy.

I remember one of the most popular talk radio hosts proclaiming that he thought it would be a good idea if we just put all the drug abusers to death—that would clean up the country! Of course he was busted for purchasing illegal prescription drugs from a drug dealer.

And then there's the litany of TV evangelists who try to keep their sins in the dark. A new one seems to get exposed for their secret sin each week.

And don't think that it doesn't happen in the Adventist Church.

Years ago I was speaking at a camp meeting with a well-known individual in our church. He is a person who can be vocally critical of a certain segment of believers.

One morning I was to pick him up for breakfast so that we could chat and get to know each other a little better. When I arrived at his room, I knocked on his door and let myself in. He was still in the shower. Those were the days before you could just order a movie on your hotel system. I noticed his VCR was still on. So I hit the eject button. The movie he rented that Friday night previous was one that the world calls "adult entertainment." I say no adult should be entertained by this kind of thing.

When he got out of the shower, he saw that I had discovered what he'd been watching. Starting to cry, he begged me not to tell anyone. He wanted to keep things in the dark, because he knew that shedding light on his sin would hurt. That it would hurt bad.

I made him promise me that he would get help and that I would follow up on the commitment. That morning he preached in the main auditorium. But not long afterward he obtained some professional counseling for his secret addiction and let the light of truth shine on his darkness. After confessing his sin to the appropriate people, he became one of the least critical leaders in our church. He knows that it's not his business to throw stones at other believers.

Another aspect of confession has to do with positive confessions.

I'm sure you've heard the story about the husband and wife who were celebrating their twenty-fifth anniversary. The wife looked at her husband and asked, "How come you never tell me you love me?"

The husband glanced back at his wife and said, "I told you I love you on our wedding day. If I change my mind, I'll let you know."

Wives need husbands to acknowledge their love to them on a regular basis both in words and in action. Those three powerful words are not to live in the darkness. It does us damage when we hide them in the darkness away from our loved ones. Some of us have experienced the premature death of a loved one and had to live with the regret of not telling them how we really felt about them.

God needs to hear it too. He longs for us to confess our love, our loyalty, and our feelings about Him. That's why worshipping Him in church and in song is so important. It gives us a chance to tell God what we think about Him in artful, beautiful, poetic ways. And it allows us to take our feelings out of the darkness and into the light.

Here's a thought that I'd like to share with you about darkness and light and confession. Maybe it is the most important thing I could say about confession: Jesus is the confessor of God.

"In the beginning was the Word, and the Word was with God, and the Word was God. He was in the beginning with God. All things were made through Him, and without Him nothing was made that was made.

In Him was life, and the life was the light of men. And the light shines in the darkness, and the darkness did not comprehend it. There was a man sent from God, whose name was John. This man came for a witness, to bear witness of the Light, that all through him might believe. He was not the Light, but was sent to bear witness of that Light. That was the true Light which gives light to every man coming into the world. He was in the world, and the world was made through Him, and the world did not know Him. He came to His own, and His own did not receive Him. But as many as received Him, to them He gave the right to become children of God, to those who believe in His name: who were born, not of blood, nor of the will of the flesh, nor of the will of man, but of God. And the Word became flesh and dwelt among us, and we beheld His glory, the glory as of the only begotten of the Father, full of grace and truth. John bore witness of Him and cried out, saying, 'This was He of whom I said, "He who comes after me is preferred before me, for He was before me."' And of His fullness we have all received, and grace for grace. For the law was given through Moses, but grace and truth came through Jesus Christ. No one has seen God at any time. The only begotten Son, who is in the bosom of the Father, He has declared Him" (John 1:1-18, NKJV).

As we have noted already, people have speculated widely about why Jesus came to earth. For example, some have said He did it so that He could die for us, and others say that He wanted to save us. I think both these and many other ideas have merit. But John 1 brings out still another aspect.

John 1 would suggest that Jesus used it as an opportunity to confess the Father. Jesus wanted to shed light on the darkness that dominated the minds of God's people about who God was. Our Savior said, "If you've seen Me, you've seen the Father."

When Jesus lit the world with a new knowledge of the Father, that light hurt many of those who had charge of the religious community. They had been living in the dark for so long that when Jesus turned the light of truth on, they couldn't take the pain. That's why Scripture describes Him as the Stone that makes human beings stumble, and the Rock that makes them fall.

So instead of seeing the light and acknowledging their sin, or confessing a new understanding of the Father, the religious leaders of the day snuffed out the light. Or at least they tried to.

People still continue their attempt to dwell in darkness. That's why it's so important for us to be light bearers in our dark world. Confessing the truth about our loving God isn't always going to be easy. Sometimes others will seek to snuff out your light. But remember, we are called into the light and not into darkness.

Our church's specific mission is to shed the light of Jesus on this world's dark view of God. Our job—our calling—is to confess the Father in the light of His Son, Jesus Christ. But that can never happen as long as we insist on keeping things hidden in the dark. The longer we harbor darkness in our secret lives, the more damage that darkness will do to us. People who cling to darkness, who try to keep their sin hidden, become people who refuse to share the light.

In Jesus' words in John 3:19-21: "This is the verdict: Light has come into the world, but people loved darkness instead of light because their deeds were evil. Everyone who does evil hates the light, and will not come into the light for fear that their deeds will be exposed. But whoever lives by the truth comes into the light, so that it may be seen plainly that what they have done has been done in the sight of God."

Our challenge as a church is to come out of the darkness and into the light. Then we in turn must light the world with Jesus' love. That can only happen if we are willing to let the light of truth shine on our own darkness. As we began to confess our darkness and be vulnerable and accountable for whom we've become, God will change us, just as He did with King David, with Peter, and with Paul.

Let's let the light of truth and confession shine in our marriages, in our homes, in our businesses, and everywhere else in our lives. It's time to put darkness away and live in the light.

CHAPTER 15

When the apostles returned, they reported to Jesus what they had done. Then he took them with him and they withdrew by themselves to a town called Bethsaida, but the crowds learned about it and followed him. He welcomed them and spoke to them about the kingdom of God, and healed those who needed healing. Late in the afternoon the Twelve came to him and said, 'Send the crowd away so they can go to the surrounding villages and countryside and find food and lodging, because we are in a remote place here.' He replied, 'You give them something to eat.' They answered, 'We have only five loaves of bread and two fish—unless we go and buy food for all this crowd.' (About five thousand men were there.) But he said to his disciples, 'Have them sit down in groups of about fifty each.' The disciples did so, and everyone sat down. Taking the five loaves and the two fish and looking up to heaven, he gave thanks and broke them. Then he gave them to the disciples to distribute to the people. They all ate and were satisfied, and the disciples picked up twelve basketfuls of broken pieces that were left over" (Luke 9:10-17).

To be honest, the first thought I had when I read this story again was that at 18 years of age I worked for Skippers Fish and Chips. I didn't have very much money back then, and employees' meals were free, so just about every day for nearly two years I ate the same thing for lunch and for supper: two pieces of fish, fries, and a bowl of coleslaw. To this day, interestingly, I like fish and chips about as much as anything there is to eat.

Jesus treated the people on the side of that hill that day to all you can eat fish and chips. I'll bet the fish tasted heavenly.

Another part of the story here that I think worth noting does not appear in Luke's version. John 6 tells where the fish and chips came from. It seems that a young boy whose mother thought ahead and packed him a lunch was willing to contribute his fish and chips to help solve the problem on that day.

I have to admire the character of a lad who would give up his food, knowing that he might go hungry until he got home later. He showed some real self-sacrifice. In fact, that little boy gave us all an example of how Jesus wants us to act. Seeing that people were hungry, he offered them something to eat. Without thinking of himself, he donated what was his to lighten the burden of others.

He could have said, "Here, Jesus, You can have one of my fish and two of my loaves of bread." Instead, he offered everything he had to the Master, and the Master did more than the child could have ever expected.

When we give our all—when we don't hold anything back from Jesus—

He is able to multiply our gift and make it something bigger than we could have ever imagined.

I think these are both great life lessons that we can take from the wonderful story of feeding the 5,000. But I find one more that, for me at least, may be the most important one, and it appears in Luke 9:12, 13.

When the disciples present Jesus with a problem, they also offer Him a solution. They say, "Let's send all the people away so that they can get something to eat."

Jesus could have told them, "You know, you're right. It's getting late, there's no 7-11 across the street, no McDonald's drive-through, so we'd better call it a night and dismiss everyone."

Yes, He could have said that, but He didn't. Instead, Jesus looked at His disciples and said, "You give them something to eat."

Can you imagine how they might have responded? Some of them must have just stared at Jesus like a deer caught in headlights. Others might have said, "Uh, Jesus, I don't have my food handlers' permit."

"Jesus, we don't even have anything to eat for ourselves, so how are we supposed to feed all these people?"

You give them something to eat. That was His response. Evidently the disciples were unaware that they had anything to offer.

I'm going to take a weird turn here just for a moment, but stay with me and you'll discover why I think the disciples didn't think they had anything worthwhile to present.

Pastor Carlton Byrd talked about this in a meeting I once attended, and it has stuck with me ever since. Six chapters after Luke 9 is another familiar story.

"There was a man who had two sons. The younger one said to his father, 'Father, give me my share of the estate.' So he divided his property between them. . . . Meanwhile, the older son was in the field. When he came near the house, he heard music and dancing. So he called one of the servants and asked him what was going on. 'Your brother has come,' he replied, 'and your father has killed the fattened calf because he has him back safe and sound.' The older brother became angry and refused to go in. So his father went out and pleaded with him. But he answered his father, 'Look! All these years I've been slaving for you and never disobeyed your orders. Yet you never gave me even a young goat so I could celebrate with my friends. But when this son of yours who has squandered your property with prostitutes comes home, you kill the fattened calf for him!' 'My son,' the father said, 'you are always with me, and everything I have is yours. But we had to celebrate and be glad, because this brother of yours was dead and is alive again; he was lost and is found'" (Luke 15:11-32).

What was the older son's problem? Was he just a killjoy? Did he not like barbecue? Or did he despise his younger brother so much that he didn't want to join the party?

I'd like to suggest to you that the older brother's difficulty was that he didn't know who he was or what he had. He was one of those people concerned about a lot of things, but not the right ones.

I had an elder in one church who expressed first in groups and then individually to me and then every other day with e-mails his concern about the music in the church, about how another elder was dressed while on the platform, about the fact that we were eating so much processed food in potluck . . . His list of concerns and the intensity of his worry was overwhelming him to the point of paralysis.

For the first four months of my tenure there I got consumed by the lists of worries and the e-mail after e-mail and the article after article he had me read to convince me of how I should be concerned too. Finally I just couldn't do it anymore. Sitting down with him, I said, "Here you are, one of the most talented and smartest people in this whole church, and you've been immobilized by all your concerns. Instead of being on the warpath to fix everything that you are afraid is going to be wrong with the church, let's actually start being proactive and do something."

"What do you mean?"

I told him that I wasn't willing to sit in an elders' meeting for three hours at a time and talk about all his issues anymore. Instead, each elders' meeting needed to be a proactive experience of planning on how to shepherd our church and bring new people into the kingdom. No more complaining and worrying in such meetings. But unable to see the point, he resigned the next month.

Have you ever met someone who became so concerned about everybody and everything around them to the point they suck the joy even out of a group of joyful people? That, I believe, was what was happening to the older son in the parable. He was so worried about himself and his status with the father that he couldn't set it all aside and celebrate with his long-lost brother.

Not only was he concerned, he was also blind. Consider what his complaint was, and then the father's response.

" 'Look! All these years I've been slaving for you and never disobeyed your orders. Yet you never gave me even a young goat so I could celebrate with my friends. But when this son of yours who has squandered your property with prostitutes comes home, you kill the fattened calf for him!' 'My son,' the father said, 'you are always with me, and everything I have is yours' " (Luke 15:29-31).

"You are my son! Everything I have is yours! I gave you everything you've ever wanted, and it's been yours all along, yet you've never done anything with it to bring you or your friends joy."

I know some people who go to church and act just like that.

One time I preached a public series on the character of God and said something that gave a few of my church members moose nostrils.

I talked about how God had written each and every person's name in the book of life even before they were born and planned on them being saved and in heaven with Him. And that if they had ever responded to the gospel of grace, or to the promptings of the Holy Spirit in their lives, they had accepted God's destiny for their lives and salvation was theirs.

It wasn't long before I got an e-mail from a church member. It detailed that we could never "know" if we are saved and that we shouldn't tell people that they are saved, and that I should never preach such things again.

The person was very concerned.

I sent an e-mail back with about 30 Bible references to the fact that God's work of salvation for us was accomplished even before the foundation of the world, and that we should stand confident in God's grace.

The response was to write a lengthy letter to my conference president. After he looked at all our e-mails, the church leader told me to keep preaching the good news of the gospel.

I believe that one of the reasons we have so many Christians that don't share their faith is that like the older son in the parable, they don't know what they already have!

Many Christians look at John 3:16 and read it as though it says, "For God so loved the world, that He gave His only begotten Son, that whosoever believeth in Him might not perish, and if that individual gets really lucky and God is in a good mood that day, maybe they'll receive eternal life, kind of, if their fingers are crossed and if they do enough to make God love them."

No wonder Christians don't share their faith! They aren't even convinced it works for them!

Our church has many older brothers who don't know who they are or what they have!

It's time that they wake up and realize their identity and what they possess. All of us are children of the King! And we have received the gift of salvation from a Father that is so crazy in love with us it keeps Him up at night!

God has given us everything—it's ours for the keeping. Now, stop being paralyzed by your concerns and do something with our gift!

Jesus sat on the side of a hill with more than 5,000 hungry people. His disciples tell Him the people need food and to send them away.

Jesus says, "You feed them."

He was trying to teach them that everything that He had, they also had access to. All that was His was theirs.

You are sons of the Father who owns the cattle on a thousand hills. Your Father owns the whole franchise for the fish and chips restaurant! And you are His sons! You feed them.

Jesus was teaching His disciples the simple lesson that God's plan for our world is for His sons and daughters to be His hands and feet here.

Stop being so concerned about the problems or potential dangers in the church and do something!

If Jesus were here, and you were to bring your concerns to Him, I'll bet you dollars to doughnuts that His response would be "All that I have is yours. You feed them."

The disciples started being waiters in the outdoor restaurant on that hill and delivered the biggest all-you-can-eat fish and chips meal in the history of the world. And afterward there were so many blessings that each disciple had a basket full of leftovers when everyone finished.

You know, that's how it works. When we finally drop the burden of our concerns and fears and realize who we are and what we've been given—when we begin to do something for God—the blessings rain down so heavily that there are leftover blessings for a need down the road.

Jesus said, "You feed them."

CHAPTER 16

Jesus and the End of Time

One of my great joys in life is eating. I love to eat. I have been known to arrange trips around restaurants that may be on the way.

I'm mostly an entrée guy. If I have the choice between getting another helping of an entrée versus having one entrée and a dessert, I'll take another helping of the entrée, please . . . Unless we are talking about rhubarb pie. Rhubarb pie is the one dessert that I would always prefer over a second helping of an entrée.

One evening my mom served us dinner and, just before we sat down, informed me that she had made rhubarb pie and had some vanilla ice cream to go with it.

I couldn't wait to race through my entrée in order to get to the rhubarb pie and ice cream. But there was one problem. On my plate next to the perfectly good food rested several little developmentally disabled cabbages, otherwise known at brussels sprouts.

I will eat almost everything. Other than the few foods I won't eat because I'm directed not to by the Bible, I like just about everything—except brussels sprouts.

Now I had a decision to make. You see, at my house one didn't get dessert unless they finished everything on their plate. The rest of the plate wasn't a problem. But standing between me and a huge helping of hot rhubarb pie and ice cream were seven round, green, bitter, mushy lumps of disgusting yuck.

For a moment I considered scooping them into a napkin and throwing them away when my parents' heads were turned. But if they caught me doing that, I would get no pie . . . ever.

After eating everything on my plate except my brussels sprouts, I then told my mom I was full, but had just enough room for dessert.

It didn't work. She reminded me of our family rule. I had to finish all of my plate before I could have dessert. If it were any other dessert I would have gladly given up my right to it. But rhubarb pie and vanilla ice cream . . .

So I sat there and tried to psych myself up to put the first of the seven little devils in my mouth. I just couldn't do it. So I sat there. An hour after everyone else had finished their dinner and their dessert I still stared at my now-lukewarm and even mushier foes.

Finally I put one of them in my mouth. It was worse than I had even imagined. Gagging, I spit it back on my plate.

We started supper at 5:00 that night. I didn't get my rhubarb pie and ice cream until 9:30. It was an epochal battle between my foes and me, but in the end the rhubarb pie was worth it.

Matthew 24 is Jesus' sermon to His disciples after they asked Him when and how the end of time would come about.

It's an amazing read, actually. Much of Jesus' time line for how history would unfold parallels John's vision of the end-time in Revelation. Jesus really parts the curtain on what we are to expect just before He comes to take us home.

Seventh-day Adventists have long been fascinated by end-time scenarios. We've created time lines as to what is going to happen so that we won't be surprised or deceived. Some have even tried to predict how other people are going to persecute us before Jesus returns.

When I was little and my mom first started attending the Adventist Church seriously, she was so obsessed with the Second Advent happening in just a short time that she bought survival books and studied them so that we could live in the wilderness during the great time of trouble. I tried to remind her that God just had crows deliver food to Elijah when he fled into the wilderness, but she didn't listen. She even made me taste a fern once.

The Second Coming, the end of time, the time of trouble—all have intrigued Seventh-day Adventists and other Christians for hundreds of years. As I've worked with Adventist publishing houses one of my editors told me that if I wanted to make money in the Adventist publishing industry I should write books about the last days.

The time period before Jesus returns just fascinates Adventists. We even spend the bulk of our public evangelistic efforts in trying to convince people that the end is imminent, so you better get in the boat while it's still at the dock!

So it's no surprise to find out that the Bible has much to say about the second coming of Jesus. I enjoy studying about the end of time too. I love the books of Daniel and Revelation and what Paul says about the Second Advent. And I love what Jesus says about it in the Gospels and especially in Matthew 24.

But I want to caution you and myself about something. I've heard someone say, "Don't be so heavenly-minded that you are no earthly good."

Another way to put it into context is with my story at the beginning of this chapter: "You don't get your pie unless you clean your plate first."

In Matthew 24 Jesus tells us all about events before His second coming. Then He reminds us that our task until that time is to be ready. That's our job. To be ready for Him to come back.

So how does one go about being ready?

Fortunately, Jesus didn't just give us a job and not tell us how to do it. He was kind enough to instruct us on what it means. We are to ready ourselves for the kingdom to come by first bringing the kingdom of God to this earth.

In fact, in the very next chapter after Matthew 24 Jesus relates to His followers three parables that explain what that involves. Now remember, when Matthew wrote his letter the divisions of chapters and verses did not yet exist. Matthew 24 flowed directly into Matthew 25.

The three parables are those of the 10 virgins, the parable of the talents, and the parable of the sheep and the goats.

So how do they teach us how to be ready for Jesus to come?

"At that time the kingdom of heaven will be like ten virgins who took their lamps and went out to meet the bridegroom. Five of them were foolish and five were wise. The foolish ones took their lamps but did not take any oil with them. The wise ones, however, took oil in jars along with their lamps. The bridegroom was a long time in coming, and they all became drowsy and fell asleep. At midnight the cry rang out: 'Here's the bridegroom! Come out to meet him!' Then all the virgins woke up and trimmed their lamps. The foolish ones said to the wise, 'Give us some of your oil; our lamps are going out.' 'No,' they replied, 'there may not be enough for both us and you. Instead, go to those who sell oil and buy some for yourselves.' But while they were on their way to buy the oil, the bridegroom arrived. The virgins who were ready went in with him to the wedding banquet. And the door was shut. Later the others also came. 'Lord, Lord' they said, 'open the door for us!' But he replied, 'Truly I tell you, I don't know you.' Therefore keep watch, because you do not know the day or the hour" (Matt. 25:1-13).

There it is, that warning to be ready. This parable has two crucial elements that I'd like to bring to your attention. One is the metaphor of oil.

We know from our Bible study that oil is synonymous with God's Spirit working in the life to transform one's character.

"Without the Spirit of God a knowledge of His word is of no avail. The theory of truth, unaccompanied by the Holy Spirit, cannot quicken the soul or sanctify the heart. One may be familiar with the commands and promises of the Bible; but unless the Spirit of God sets the truth home, the character will not be transformed" (Ellen G. White, *Christ's Object Lessons,* p. 408).

In other words, we can be as right as right can be—can stand on the firm truth of every sure doctrine and argue the truth as we see it until the cows come home—but if we aren't allowing God to transform us every day to be more and more like Jesus, we are like a resounding gong or a clanging cymbal.

"If we would humble ourselves before God, and be kind and courteous and tenderhearted and pitiful, there would be one hundred conversions to the truth where now there is only one. But, though professing to be converted, we carry around with us a bundle of self that we regard as altogether too precious to be given up. It is our privilege to lay this burden at the feet of Christ and in its place take the character and similitude of Christ. The Saviour is waiting for us to do this" (Ellen G. White, *Testimonies for the Church,* vol. 9, pp. 189, 190).

God would have us lay our insatiable desire to be right at the foot of the cross and allow Him to replace that with a character that is pliable and tenderhearted toward one another and with the people we come in contact with.

The other part of the parable I consider especially worth noting is that the five wise virgins had prepared for the long haul. They suspected that the bridegroom was not going to arrive too quickly. (Even today, important figures in Middle Eastern culture do not do things until they are ready. They do not follow strict schedules or rush through things. Events happen only when they get around to them and not until then.) So the wise virgins prepared for a long wait.

I think we need to get it in our heads that being ready for Jesus to come means that we need to be ready on *this earth.* We may be here a while. So while we are here, what kind of people should we be? How should we treat one another? How should we relate to the world?

The second parable in Matthew 25 is that of the talents. In it a wealthy man, before he goes on a journey, leaves investment money with three people who work for him. When he returns, he brings the three men in to see what they have accomplished with his money. The first one invested the funds and got a good return, as did the second guy. But the third one had just buried it in the ground, the master of the house thus receiving only the original sum back.

So how can this particular parable teach us to be ready for Jesus' return? Notice the reaction of the third servant, the one who wasn't "ready."

"Then the man who had received one bag of gold came. 'Master,' he said, 'I knew that you are a hard man, harvesting where you have not sown and gathering where you have not scattered seed. So I was afraid and went out and hid your gold in the ground. See, here is what belongs to you' " (Matt. 25:24, 25).

He thought he knew what God's character was like, and he painted the Father as a hard man. His fear of God drove him to act as he did.

Jesus, elsewhere in Matthew, proclaims that "not everyone who says to me, 'Lord, Lord,' will enter the kingdom of heaven, but only the one who does the will of my Father who is in heaven. Many will say to me on that day, 'Lord, Lord, did we not prophesy in your name and in your name drive out demons and in your name perform many miracles?' Then I will tell them plainly, 'I never knew you. Away from me, you evildoers!' " (Matt. 7:21-23).

And why does the Father call them "evildoers"? Because they believe that God is merciless, exacting, a "I'm right and you are wrong" prideful deity, they serve Him in ways that reflect what they think He is like. But consider this:

"The last rays of merciful light, the last message of mercy to be given to the world, is a revelation of His character of love. The children of God are to manifest His glory. In their own life and character they are to reveal what the grace of God has done for them" (Ellen G. White, *Christ's Object Lessons,* pp. 415, 416).

The people that God cannot allow into the kingdom have forgotten that He is a Deity of love. They no longer remember that in Acts 1:11 angels remind the disciples, as they look up in the air at the ascending Jesus, that this same Jesus would come back to get us. The loving, kind, considerate Jesus they had come to know would return exactly as He had been. So until then, we are to emulate Him as we interact with one another.

And finally, that third parable: the sheep and the goats.

"When the Son of Man comes in his glory, and all the angels with him, he will sit on his glorious throne. All the nations will be gathered before him, and he will separate the people one from another as a shepherd separates the sheep from the goats. He will put the sheep on his right and the goats on his left. Then the King will say to those on his right, 'Come, you who are blessed by my Father; take your inheritance, the kingdom prepared for you since the creation of the world. For I was hungry and you gave me something to eat, I was thirsty and you gave me something to drink, I was a stranger and you invited me in, I needed clothes and you clothed me, I was sick and you looked after me, I was in prison and you came to visit me.' Then the righteous will answer him, 'Lord, when did we see you hungry and feed you, or thirsty and give you something to drink? When did we see you a stranger and invite you in, or needing clothes and clothe you? When did we see you sick or in prison and go to visit you?' The King will reply, 'Truly I tell you, whatever you did for one of the least of these brothers and sisters of mine, you did for me.' Then he will say to those on his left, 'Depart from me, you who are cursed, into the eternal fire prepared for the devil and his angels. For I was hungry and you gave me nothing to eat, I was thirsty and you gave me nothing to drink, I was a stranger and you did not invite me in, I needed clothes and you did not clothe me, I was sick and in prison and you did not look after me.' They also will answer, 'Lord, when did we see you hungry or thirsty or a stranger or needing clothes or sick or in prison, and did not help you?' He will reply, 'Truly I tell you, whatever you did not do for one of the least of these, you did not do for me.' Then they will go away to eternal punishment, but the righteous to eternal life" (Matt. 25:31-46).

The final way that we can be ready for Jesus' second coming is to be found doing His work when He returns. And His work, according to His own words, is for us to be His hands and feet in the lives of the less fortunate in our sphere of influence.

"The strongest argument in favor of the gospel is a loving and lovable Christian" (Ellen G. White, *The Ministry of Healing,* p. 470).

God calls us to be compassionate with one another and with the world. Yes, He expects us to pray for one another, but also to follow up those prayers with hands and feet doing the business of Jesus. Touching people with His touch, and doing this in the realization that as we help people, we are actually serving Jesus Himself.

"Christ is waiting with longing desire for the manifestation of Himself in His church. When the character of Christ shall be perfectly reproduced in His people, then He will come to claim them as His own" (Ellen G. White, *Christ's Object Lessons,* p. 69).

This famous quote penned by Ellen White when read in context tells us that we need to learn to be lovers of one another and lovers of those we come in contact with every day. That's what it means to have the character of Christ perfectly reproduced in us.

Jesus is coming soon. That's the dessert. But we have work to do on earth before we get to our dessert. While we wait, God asks us to be ready.

And being ready means that when He does come back, He will find us doing the work of God.

Oh, and if we take part in His work, we will discover that it doesn't go down like brussels sprouts. Rather, if we partner with God on earth, we will find out that it's like eating two desserts. And what could be better than that?

CHAPTER **17**

Jesus Is Our Shepherd

Once every thousand years or so somebody writes something down that is so profound it lasts for centuries. Biblically speaking, a select few passages seem to transcend religious dogma and even the Christian faith: the Ten Commandments; John 3:16; 1 Corinthians 13; and the twenty-third psalm. The twenty-third psalm is the second most memorized part of the Bible, right after John 3:16. And if you're like me, you memorized it in the King James Version. It almost doesn't sound right if it's not recited in the language of the KJV, does it?

"The Lord is my shepherd; I shall not want.

He maketh me to lie down in green pastures:

he leadeth me beside the still waters.

He restoreth my soul:

he leadeth me in the paths of righteousness for his name's sake.

Yea, though I walk through the valley of the shadow of death, I will fear no evil:

for thou art with me; thy rod and thy staff they comfort me.

Thou preparest a table before me in the presence of mine enemies: thou anointest my head with oil; my cup runneth over.

Surely goodness and mercy shall follow me all the days of my life: and I will dwell in the house of the Lord for ever."

"The Lord is my shepherd."

That's quite a statement. If a person really means the words, what are they actually saying? What kind of trust are they placing in God if they are truly allowing Him to be their Shepherd?

I love to guide white-water rafting adventures. But I wasn't always a guide. I remember the first time I boarded a raft and placed my life in the hands of Mark Hylarides. Mark had been a guide for several years before I got in the boat with him. But I had never been white-water rafting. I had never seen him guide a boat. And I'm not the strongest swimmer in the world.

I can still see myself sitting there on the side of the raft before our trip. Despite the fact that I had my wet suit on, my life jacket secured, and my paddle in my hand, I was as unsure about this white water adventure as anything I had ever done.

Before we launched in the river Mark gave us what he deemed a "safety talk." He told us what to do if the raft flipped over in the white water or we found ourselves caught in rapids and the raft started to get sucked into a hydraulic (situations in which water coursing over an obstruction flows backward and can trap the raft under the surface of the water). He explained what to do if we fell out of the raft into the glacier-cold water.

By the time he was winding up his talk I wasn't sure I wanted to go white-water rafting anymore. Maybe it wasn't my spiritual calling.

Finally, with a firm, confident, friendly voice he said, "Listen to me. If you just listen to your guide and do everything your guide tells you to do, even if you get into some trouble, you'll be fine."

Just pay attention to your guide and you'll be fine.

Jesus said, "My sheep listen to my voice; I know them, and they follow me. I give them eternal life, and they shall never perish; no one can snatch them out of my hand. My Father, who has given them to me, is greater than all; no one can snatch them out of my Father's hand. I and the Father are one" (John 10:27-30).

I think one of the problems with listening to our Guide, our Shepherd, is that sometimes we don't recognize His voice.

We always have some people in our lives whose voice we can identify without having to see them. Whether on the phone or heard from another room, when they speak, we recognize their voice, because we have spent time with them.

Can we say the same thing about Jesus? I realize that most of us have knowledge about Him, but do we *know* Him? Do we spend so much time with Jesus that we recognize His voice when He speaks to us?

To further press the issue, is our life so busy with good things that we don't take the time to listen to hear if Jesus is even speaking to us? Do we know the voice of our Shepherd?

"He maketh me to lie down in green pastures: he leadeth me beside the still waters. He restoreth my soul."

Doesn't that image just look restful? "He maketh me to lie down in green pastures." It's the picture of contentment, isn't it? Have you had those days when everything just seemed to be right?

But look at how these two verses are connected. "He maketh me to lie down in green pastures: he leadeth me beside the still waters. He restoreth my soul."

If the Good Shepherd has to restore my soul, what does that presuppose? That before I followed the Shepherd into the green pastures and by the still waters my soul needed some mending, some healing.

Have you ever needed the Good Shepherd to lead you to green pastures and to still waters to restore your soul? I have.

About 20 years ago I was the chaplain for what was then called Canadian Union College. To say that I was the chaplain of the college is an understatement at best. My actual job description was to be the chaplain of the college, the chaplain of the academy, and the associate pastor of the church. They also asked me to be the coach of the girls' volleyball team in my spare time.

To add to my duties, I got the brilliant idea that I should get a master's degree in marriage and family therapy. After all, I didn't have anything else to do, so . . .

It was February, I didn't like my job or the weather, and I was knee-deep in a master's degree program that required me to start some supervised counseling. During those counseling sessions I began hearing things that I was not prepared for—gut-wrenching and horrifying things that adults did to people they were supposed to protect.

The job, the counseling sessions, and everything else piled up so that, unbeknownst to me, my soul had a bloody nose.

I remember after one rough weekend I woke up on a Sunday morning with just enough energy to drag myself out of bed and get a bowl of cereal. My wife was in the living room watching TV.

Sitting on the couch, I started eating my Cheerios. I barely had the energy to get the spoon to my mouth. When I was about halfway through my cereal, Wendy glanced at me and, with a shocked expression on her face, said, "Sweetheart, what's the matter?"

Evidently tears were streaming down my face, and I didn't even know it. I was a wreck.

Have you ever needed Jesus to breathe life back into your weary soul?

He gives us an open invitation: "Come to me, all you who are weary and burdened, and I will give you rest" (Matt. 11:28).

God knows that this world will maul us. I think that's one reason that He gave us the wonderful gift of Sabbath.

The Sabbath is our once-a-week soul restorer. It's the one time a week we should be able to put all the soul-wrecking, soul-damaging, soul-straining activities behind us and let the Lord do some badly needed healing of our souls.

The third angel's message in Revelation 14 describes those who follow the beast as those who have "no rest day or night" (verse 11). They are people with perpetually wrecked souls.

I know quite a few Seventh-day Adventists that have forfeited the rest of the Sabbath for what they would deem as necessary activity. God gave you the gift of the Sabbath for soul repair. Use that gift.

"He leadeth me in the paths of righteousness for his name's sake."

It's interesting that we tend to make everything about us. We become Christians so that we can go to heaven. We follow Jesus because of what's in it for us.

The Bible actually looks at salvation differently than we do. Scripture declares that God gives us grace, saves us, and leads us to do righteous acts, *for His name's sake.*

It's the job of His people to make Him look good! That's why the third commandment is a huge part of the ten: "Thou shalt not take the name of the Lord thy God in vain; for the Lord will not hold him guiltless that taketh his name in vain" (Ex. 20:7, KJV).

When we proclaim ourselves as Christians but act like the devil, we misrepresent God. We make Him look bad!

The opposite is true also. When we say that we are believers and act like God, it makes Him look good. That's why the psalmist declares, "He leadeth me in the paths of righteousness *for his name's sake.*"

"Yea, though I walk through the valley of the shadow of death, I will fear no evil: for thou art with me; thy rod and thy staff they comfort me. Thou preparest a table before me in the presence of mine enemies: thou anointest my head with oil; my cup runneth over."

I love how King David writes this part of the psalm. He seems almost to take confident delight in walking through the valley of the shadow of death and sitting at a table with his enemies. He acknowledges that there are going to be occasions in life when we are paddling upstream, when we are biking against the wind, when times will be dark.

That first time I went rafting, the water was smooth for the first part of our trip. It was very pleasant. And then we hit a series of white water that was so violent, I didn't know if we were going to make it through. In fact, right after we hit the first hole, I fell out of the raft.

But as soon as I did, I felt a hand grab mine. It was my guide. And he pulled me back into the boat. He didn't make the white water go away. But he guided me safely through it. And you know what, even though it was scary, he made the journey almost enjoyable.

All of us have had our share of walking through the valley of the shadow of death. But we do not travel alone. Our Shepherd is with us, guiding us, and He can even make the journey through those valleys enjoyable—if we let Him. Remember, Jesus says, "I will never leave you, or forsake you."

"Surely goodness and mercy shall follow me all the days of my life: and I will dwell in the house of the Lord for ever."

The twenty-third psalm almost seems to depict our life journey, doesn't it? We will have times of peace and times of trouble. All the way along life's path, and if we are willing, our Shepherd will guide us. And in the end? We will dwell in the house of the Lord forever.

It's interesting that we as sheep have it as our goal to dwell eternally in the Lord's house. We can get very busy trying to reach that goal. What we forget is that the Shepherd is the one who will guide us safely home. It's not the job of sheep to shepherd themselves, but rather that of the Shepherd. And it's His desire to keep His sheep safe until they are home with Him.

CHAPTER **18**

Jesus and the Hypocrites

A long time ago war shattered the peace of heaven.

"And there was war in heaven, Michael and his angels waging war with the dragon. The dragon and his angels waged war, and they were not strong enough, and there was no longer a place found for them in heaven. And the great dragon was thrown down, the serpent of old who is called the devil and Satan, who deceives the whole world" (Rev. 12:7-9, NASB).

This dragon serpent, this once bright and morning star, became the deceiver of the whole world. He misled Adam and Eve. And according to the Bible, his plan is to trick you and me.

As the story in the Bible continues to play out we see that he has implanted in human hearts everywhere the drive to put themselves first and others last. He has made it the norm for people to be filled with pride and selfishness.

Through prophecy we learn that there would arise a religious power that the Bible calls the little horn. It would have all of the allure and trappings of religion, but would actually do damage to the name of God and persecute those who would dare stand up against it.

But the little-horn power will not be alone. "Then I saw another beast coming up out of the earth; and he had two horns like a lamb and he spoke as a dragon. He exercises all the authority of the first beast in his presence. And he makes the earth and those who dwell in it to worship the first beast, whose fatal wound was healed. He performs great signs, so that he even makes fire come down out of heaven to the earth in the presence of men" (Rev. 13:11-13, NASB).

This second power will resemble a lamb, but speak like a dragon. Who is the lamb? Jesus. Who is the dragon? Satan. The new entity will be a wolf dressed in sheep's clothing, something that seems really good on the outside, but on the inside . . .

It will seemingly perform miracles to the point of calling fire down from heaven! When you think of the miracle of fire pouring down from heaven, what does it remind you of in the Bible? Elijah?

But there is still another place in the Bible where fire streams down from heaven. Acts 2 records one of the greatest miracles in the Bible. It involves tongues of fire that flash down from heaven and land on the heads of all the praying believers. They rush out of their room and start speaking to the international crowd of people there for the festival in Jerusalem. All of the people hear what the disciples of Christ are preaching in their own language. Quite a miracle.

Is it possible that this religious power that looks like the Lamb, but speaks like a dragon, will counterfeit Acts 2 and turn it from something that blesses others into a "miracle" that only edifies oneself?

On the Sermon on the Mount, Jesus warns us of such a danger: "Watch out for false prophets. They come to you in sheep's clothing, but inwardly they are ferocious wolves. By their fruit you will recognize them. Do people pick grapes from thornbushes, or figs from thistles? Likewise, every good tree bears good fruit, but a bad tree bears bad fruit. A good tree cannot bear bad fruit, and a bad tree cannot bear good fruit. Every tree that does not bear good fruit is cut down and thrown into the fire. Thus, by their fruit you will recognize them. Not everyone who says to me, 'Lord, Lord,' will enter the kingdom of heaven, but only the one who does the will of my Father who is in heaven. Many will say to me on that day, 'Lord, Lord, did we not prophesy in your name and in your name drive out demons and in your name perform many miracles?' Then I will tell them plainly, 'I never knew you. Away from me, you evildoers!'" (Matt. 7:15-23).

I have a peach tree in my yard in Wenatchee. It grows like a weed. I can prune that thing back to nothing, and it will still be overloaded with peaches.

But my tree has a problem. It's infested with earwigs. Every year I would go to pick a big, juicy, ripe peach from it, break it open with my thumbs, and to my dismay, find an earwig in it that had done irreparable damage. The fruit looked so good on the outside, but the inside was horrible.

We could say something similar about the cookies a student of mine baked once upon a time.

I used to be the boys' dean at Bella Coola Adventist Academy in British Columbia about 600 miles northwest of Vancouver. I had charge of about 20 guys.

Right next to the boys' dormitory was the girls'. And they loved to bake goodies. They would make cakes and pies and cookies. The smell coming from their kitchen would often waft into the boys' dorm, tempting the poor, weak young men to sneak over and snatch whatever was cooling down on the windowsill at the girls' dorm.

And I have to admit, they succumbed to temptation more than once. They would sneak over to steal the occasional pie or a handful of freshly-baked cookies.

Naturally, that did not please the young women baking the goodies, and they would chastise the guys and tell them that if they didn't stop stealing cookies they'd be sorry. The boys would laugh it off and continue their shenanigans. Until one day . . .

One of the girls decided enough was enough. She walked out into the woods next to the dorm and collected a little bag of evidence that deer had left behind. Some would call it a bag of scat.

Then she went back to the dorm and mixed the deer scat in with her cookie dough. She baked beautiful-looking chocolate-chip cookies that day and put them out on the windowsill to cool.

Sure enough, a couple guys slipped over to the dorm and collected a good portion of those cookies and brought their trophies back over to share with the rest of the boys in the dorm.

That night in the cafeteria while everybody was eating supper, the girl that baked the cookies stood up and said, "Did you guys enjoy your cookies today?"

The boys kind of snickered, not wanting to admit to their crime. Then she held up a little baggie of what appeared to be chocolate-covered almonds.

"Well, I hope you enjoyed all of them. Because this was one of the ingredients."

She threw the bag of deer scat on the table in front of the two boys who had done the thieving that day. Their eyes got as big as saucers.

"From now on," she continued, "you will never know what's in the things we bake at the girls' dorm." That was the last time any of the boys stole anything off that windowsill.

Looked good on the outside, but rotten on the inside.

Jesus talked about a similar circumstance, only He had in mind people and not peaches or cookies.

Have you ever known somebody that behaved holy in front of all the right people, but you knew it was just an act? Or have you ever felt as if you were performing a part so that your heart wouldn't be found out?

Jesus had a particular problem with religious leaders who were beautiful on the outside but rotten on the inside. "Then Jesus said to the crowds and to his disciples: 'The teachers of the law and the Pharisees sit in Moses' seat. So you must be careful to do everything they tell you. But do not do what they do, for they do not practice what they preach. They tie up heavy, cumbersome loads and put them on other people's shoulders, but they themselves are not willing to lift a finger to move them. Everything they do is done for men to see: They make their phylacteries wide and the tassels on their garments long; they love the place of honor at banquets and the most important seats in the synagogues; they love to be greeted in the marketplaces and to be called "Rabbi" by others. . . . 'Woe to you, teachers of the law and Pharisees, you hypocrites! You travel over land and sea to win a single convert, and you have succeeded, you make them twice as much a child of hell as you are. Woe to you, teachers of the law and Pharisees, you hypocrites! You give a tenth of your spices—mint, dill and cumin. But you have neglected the more important matters of the law—justice, mercy and faithfulness. You should have practiced the latter, without neglecting the former. You blind guides! You strain out a gnat but swallow a camel. Woe to you, teachers of the law and Pharisees, you hypocrites! You clean the outside of the cup and dish, but inside they are full of greed and self-indulgence. Blind Pharisee! First clean the inside of the cup and dish, and then the outside also will be clean. Woe to you, teachers of the law and Pharisees, you hypocrites! You are like whitewashed tombs, which look beautiful on the outside but on the inside are full of the bones of the dead and everything unclean. In the same way, on the outside you appear to people as righteous but on the inside you are full of hypocrisy and wickedness'" (Matt. 23:1-28).

What was happening here with the Pharisees that got Jesus so upset? They were going to church, worshipping God, paying tithe, observing the law, and winning converts. And they were just about perfect! Just ask them!

Remember Jesus' words: "Not everyone who says to me, 'Lord, Lord,' will enter the kingdom of heaven, but only the one who does the will of my Father who is in heaven. Many will say to me on that day, 'Lord, Lord, did we not prophesy in your name and in your name drive out demons in your name and perform many miracles?' Then I will tell them plainly, 'I never knew you. Away from me, you evildoers!'" (Matt. 7:21-23).

It seems that in the end Jesus will not recognize a lot of religious people. Why? What is it that they are doing wrong? How could they be so deceived? And deceived they will be.

In fact, the Bible says that we have the possibility of understanding God in such a poor light that we will . . . well, let's let Jesus' words speak for themselves: "All this I have told you so that you will not fall away. They will put you out of the synagogue; in fact, a time is coming when anyone who kills you will think they are offering a service to God. They will do such things because they have not known the Father or me" (John 16:1-3).

We have seen this happen, haven't we? Religious history records times the church itself would burn other believers at the stake because they wouldn't do what they were told to do or believe what they were told to believe.

And even today we have people flying airplanes into buildings to kill people in the name of God, thinking that they are doing Him a service.

Wolves in sheep's clothing. Whitewashed tombs. They have not known the Father or Jesus.

A good tree will bear good fruit, and a bad tree will bear bad fruit. How do I become and stay a good tree?

I need to strive to know the Father and to know Jesus, don't I? And the only way I know to do that is to follow Jesus wherever He leads me. I need to spend time with my Savior each and every day. To avoid becoming a wolf in sheep's clothing, I must learn what Jesus would do, how He would act in every situation. I need Jesus to live in me.

The Sermon on the Mount is Jesus' attempt to teach His followers what it looks like to follow Him. He attempts to take religion out of our hands and place it gently in our hearts, so that our every breath, our every step, our every action is Spirit-led and Spirit-filled.

CHAPTER **19**

Every year my church in Burlington, Washington, would do something that, for me, was an annual life-changer. Starting on a Sabbath afternoon we would read the Bible out loud from cover to cover, ending on Friday evening.

What a moving experience it was to hear the story of God and humanity from beginning to end. As I read and as I listened I felt myself moved from elation to sadness to wonder and to frustration. I heard people laugh and sigh, and I had a few people say, “Pastor, do I have to read this out loud?”

As we got into the Gospels a few sections of Scripture particularly interested me:

“Now large crowds were going along with Him; and He turned and said to them, ‘If anyone comes to Me, and does not hate his own father and mother and wife and children and brothers and sisters, yes, and even his own life, he cannot be My disciple. Whoever does not carry his own cross and come after Me cannot be My disciple. For which one of you, when he wants to build a tower, does not first sit down and calculate the cost to see if he has enough to complete it? Otherwise, when he has laid a foundation and is not able to finish, all who observe it begin to ridicule him, saying, “This man began to build and was not able to finish.” Or what king, when he sets out to meet another king in battle, will not first sit down and consider whether he is strong enough with ten thousand men to encounter the one coming against him with twenty thousand? Or else, while the other is still far away, he sends a delegation and asks for terms of peace. So then, none of you can be My disciple who does not give up all his own possessions. Therefore, salt is good; but if even salt has become tasteless, with what will it be seasoned? It is useless either for the soil or for the manure pile; it is thrown out. He who has ears to hear, let him hear’ ” (Luke 14:25-35, NASB).

Here’s another one . . .

“Do not think that I came to bring peace on the earth; I did not come to bring peace, but a sword. For I came to set a man against his father, and a daughter against her mother, and a daughter-in-law against her mother-in-law; and a man’s enemies will be the members of his household. He who loves father or mother more than Me is not worthy of Me; and he who loves son or daughter more than Me is not worthy of Me. And he who does not take his cross and follow after Me is not worthy of Me. He who has found his life will lose it, and he who has lost his life for My sake will find it” (Matt. 10:34-39, NASB).

When we think of Jesus and His ministry here on earth our thoughts don't usually turn to these particular verses, do they? We view Him as the great uniter, healer, and restorer, but not Jesus the divider.

So what is He saying here? What's His message to you and I as we read these often-skipped-over sections of the Gospels?

These parts of the Bible always create questions in my mind: What is it exactly that Jesus wants from me? What is it that I need to do, or give up, if I want to go to heaven someday?

A couple people in the Bible actually asked Jesus that: "A certain ruler asked him, 'Good teacher, what must I do to inherit eternal life?' 'Why do you call me good?' Jesus answered. 'No one is good—except God alone. You know the commandments: "You shall not commit adultery, you shall not murder, you shall not steal, you shall not give false testimony, honor your father and mother." ' 'All these I have kept since I was a boy,' he said. When Jesus heard this, he said to him, 'You still lack one thing. Sell everything you have and give to the poor, and you will have treasure in heaven. Then come, follow me.' When he heard this, he became very sad, because he was very wealthy. Jesus looked at him and said, 'How hard it is for the rich to enter the kingdom of God! Indeed, it is easier for a camel to go through the eye of a needle than for someone who is rich to enter the kingdom of God.' Those who heard this asked, 'Who then can be saved?' Jesus replied, 'What is impossible with men is possible with God' " (Luke 18:18-27).

Great. So Jesus wants my money—all of it. I knew it. Every time I go to church all they are after is my money. Well, not so fast.

Still another person in the Bible raised the exact same question as in Luke 18, but this time Jesus gave him a completely different answer: "On one occasion an expert in the law stood up to test Jesus. 'Teacher,' he asked, 'what must I do to inherit eternal life?' 'What is written in the Law?' he replied. 'How do you read it?' He answered, ' "Love the Lord your God with all your heart and with all your soul and with all your strength and with all your mind"; and, "Love your neighbor as yourself." ' 'You have answered correctly,' Jesus replied. 'Do this and you will live.' But he wanted to justify himself, so he asked Jesus, 'And who is my neighbor?' In reply Jesus said: 'A man was going down from Jerusalem to Jericho, when he was attacked by robbers. They stripped him of his clothes, beat him and went away, leaving him half dead. A priest happened to be going down the same road, and when he saw the man, he passed by on the other side. So too, a Levite, when he came to the place and saw him, passed by on the other side. But a

Samaritan, as he traveled, came where the man was; and when he saw him, he took pity on him. He went to him and bandaged his wounds, pouring on oil and wine. Then he put the man on his own donkey, brought him to an inn and took care of him. The next day he took out two denarii and gave them to the innkeeper. "Look after him," he said, "and when I return, I will reimburse you for any extra expense you may have." Which of these three do you think was a neighbor to the man who fell into the hands of robbers?' The expert in the law replied, 'The one who had mercy on him.' Jesus told him, 'Go and do likewise'" (Luke 10:25-37).

So, then, what does Jesus want from me? He asks me to give poor people all my money, and He wants me to be nice to people whom I don't even want to associate with. Is that what these two stories mean?

Again, I ask the question What does Jesus want from me?

Contrast these two stories' people inquiring about what they needed to do or give up if they wanted to have eternal life with a couple more incidents found in the Bible:

"And He looked up and saw the rich putting their gifts into the treasury. And He saw a poor widow putting in two small copper coins. And He said, 'Truly I say to you, this poor widow put in more than all of them; for they all out of their surplus put into the offering; but she out of her poverty put in all that she had to live on'" (Luke 21:1-4, NASB).

Jesus observed the widow giving her all and praised her for her gift—in sharp contrast to what He said about people making much larger gifts into the Temple treasury.

Now consider another wonderful story from Scripture. The prophet Elijah has fled a wicked king and queen who wanted his head on a platter. He's searching for a place to stay and food to eat.

"So he went to Zarephath. When he came to the town gate, a widow was there gathering sticks. He called to her and asked, 'Would you bring me a little water in a jar so I may have a drink?' As she was going to get it, he called, 'And bring me, please, a piece of bread.' 'As surely as the Lord your God lives,' she replied, 'I don't have any bread—only a handful of flour in a jar and a little oil in a jug. I am gathering a few sticks to take home and make a meal for myself and my son, that we may eat it—and die.' Elijah said to her, 'Don't be afraid. Go home and do as you have said. But first make a small loaf of bread for me from what you have and bring it to me, and then make something for yourself and your son. For this is what the Lord, the God of Israel, says: "The jar of flour will not be used up and the jug of oil will not run dry until the day the Lord gives rain on the land."' She went away and did as Elijah had told her. So there was food every day for Elijah and for the woman and her family. For the jar of flour was not used up and the jug of oil did not run dry, in keeping with the word of the Lord spoken by Elijah" (1 Kings 17:10-16).

Here is a woman who is so destitute that she prepares to make what she believes will be her last meal, but God asks her to exhibit enough faith to use the last little bit of food on Him rather than on she and her only son.

"Oh, and if you do, I'll make sure you will never go hungry again." Right.

I wonder if she thought, *What kind of nerve does God have to ask me for my last little bit of food? Where was He when my husband got sick and died? Where has He been when my son and I went to bed hungry each night? And now He wants my last little bit of food? That's some demanding God.*

It must have taken an amazing amount of faith for that little widow to mix that last batch of bread—the only food she had left—cook it, and hand it to the prophet. But she did it. And God rewarded her for her faith.

What, then, does Jesus want from me?

Here's my simple answer to that question: Jesus asks for our all—He wants everything. He doesn't want a part-time lover—He longs for a full commitment. Nor does He desire just some of your money, but all of it as well as your body and your time and your relationships and your hobbies and your heart. Jesus wants it all.

"Hear, O Israel: The Lord our God, the Lord is one. Love the Lord your God with all your heart and with all your soul and with all your strength. These commandments that I give you today are to be on your hearts. Impress them on your children. Talk about them when you sit at home and when you walk along the road, when you lie down and when you get up. Tie them as symbols on your hands and bind them on your foreheads. Write them on the doorframes of your houses and on your gates" (Deut. 6:4-9).

What, then, does Jesus want from me? Everything.

No story in Scripture better illustrates this than that of Abraham. When God first approaches the patriarch, He gives him a promise and makes a request.

The promise is that the man will become a great nation—that is, he will have kids. The request is that Abraham pick up and leave his family, his country, and everything he knows, and move to a destination that God will reveal to him only when he arrives there. In an amazing act of faith, Abraham gets up and leaves.

But as we read the story in the book of Genesis we see that Abraham's journey of faith is all about submitting one thing after another to God's rule. Finally, in one of the stranger conversations between a human being and God ever recorded in Scripture, we come to Genesis 17. Abraham has trusted God enough to move to a strange country, and he's further demonstrated that trust in God by tithing from his increase. But Abraham fails to trust the Lord in one part of his life . . . and that's the one thing that God wants to have control of: Abraham doesn't trust that God will provide him with a son.

After all, both he and Sarah are old. They've been trying to have children for years, and nothing has been happening. Then he tries to adopt his head servant as an heir, but God says no to the idea. Next he sleeps with an Egyptian woman servant and has a child by her. Again God says no. Instead, God repeats that Sarah is going to have his child. The claim makes Abraham laugh.

So God establishes a physical reminder that Abraham needs to trust God with absolutely everything—the Lord God gives Abraham the covenant of circumcision.

God says, "Abraham, you show that you trust Me with your money by giving me a tithe of it. Now I will require a tithe of your very body. Circumcise yourself so that every time you look down you will be reminded that you must trust Me with everything."

Consider what happens when Abraham learns to trust God with everything. See how the Lord God provides. "Now the Lord was gracious to Sarah as he had said, and the Lord did for Sarah what he had promised. Sarah became pregnant and bore a son to Abraham in his old age, at the very time God had promised him. Abraham gave the name Isaac to the son Sarah bore him. When his son Isaac was eight days old, Abraham circumcised him, as God commanded him. Abraham was a hundred years old when his son Isaac was born to him" (Gen. 21:1-5).

Abraham did learn to trust God, but it was a journey of faith, just like the one you and I are on. But Abraham wasn't done with his incredible journey, was he?

Fourteen years after the birth of Isaac, God again visited Abraham and made the most outlandish request that anyone could ever ask of a human being. "Abraham, I want you to take you son to a high place, make a big pile of stones, tie your son up, lay him on that pile of stones, cut his throat, and burn him as a sacrifice to Me."

Can you imagine that? After all that he's been through to get Isaac in the first place, now the Lord orders him to slaughter him and burn him as a sacrifice? If you or I were to receive a message from God like this, I'm pretty sure we'd check ourselves in to a loony bin! Clearly we must have been hallucinating to hear such a thing.

Yet in this story, for the first time in his life, we don't see Abraham wavering in his faith. He does what the Lord requests of him. No questions. He just trusts. And once again the Lord provides.

Jesus wants our everything. He seeks our body, our work, our time, our TV, our time in the car, our sleep, our marriage, our relationships, our food, our money, our church life, and our children. Jesus wants our all.

And what gives Jesus the right to ask for our all?

He gave His all so that He could ask us for our all, so that He could give us everything in return. When we give Him our all, which in the scope of things really isn't very much, the return we get for our investment . . . well, let's just say it's worth it.

CHAPTER **20**

Jesus Wants Your Money

So here we are sitting on the side of a mountain with Jesus. We're listening to Him tell us what it looks like to be a God follower. And He's saying such things as "God followers are the salt of the earth, and they are a light on a hill." "God followers realize that it's not just what people see on the outside that counts—it's what's found on the inside, too." "God followers are people who pray and fast for the right reasons, and they keep their spiritual disciplines between them and God and don't have to make a big show of things to attract attention to themselves." "God followers realize that it's not about them—it's about giving glory and honor to God."

And then Jesus declares, "Do not store up for yourselves treasures on earth, where moths and vermin destroy, and where thieves break in and steal. But store up for yourselves treasures in heaven, where moths and vermin do not destroy, and where thieves do not break in and steal. For where your treasure is, there your heart will be also. The eye is the lamp of the body. If your eyes are healthy, your whole body will be full of light. But if your eyes are unhealthy, your whole body will be full of darkness. If then the light within you is darkness, how great is that darkness! No one can serve two masters. Either you will hate the one and love the other, or you will be devoted to the one and despise the other. You cannot serve both God and money. Therefore I tell you, do not worry about your life, what you will eat or drink; or about your body, what you will wear. Is not life more important than food, and the body more important than clothes? Look at the birds of the air; they do not sow or reap or store away in barns, and yet your heavenly Father feeds them. Are you not much more valuable than they? Can anyone of you by worrying add a single hour to your life? And why do you worry about clothes? See how the lilies of the field grow. They do not labor or spin. Yet I tell you that not even Solomon in all his splendor was dressed like one of these. If that is how God clothes the grass of the field, which is here today and tomorrow is thrown into the fire, will he not much more clothe you—you of little faith? So do not worry, saying, 'What shall we eat?' or 'What shall we drink?' or 'What shall we wear?' For the pagans run after all these things, and your heavenly Father knows that you need them. But seek first his kingdom and his righteousness, and all these things will be given to you as well. Therefore do not worry about tomorrow, for tomorrow will worry about itself. Each day has enough trouble of its own" (Matt. 6:19-34).

We looked at Jesus' wanting our money in the previous chapter. But let us go a little deeper into the issue and consider still another aspect of it.

After all, let's be honest and admit that it is a very sensitive topic. It seems as if every time I turn on a television on Sunday morning I can find a preacher on TV telling me what I should be doing with my money. Every church service seems to have a segment that involves money as a part of it.

I feel guilty every time that offering plate comes by. Why do they have to do that? Why can't I just come to church and get a blessing without those people asking me for my money all the time?

Actually, I'm convinced after studying this passage that Jesus isn't so much talking about money here as He is about priorities and about trust.

You can measure a person's priorities in several ways. One way is by examining how they choose to spend their time. For most individuals, you can watch them and determine whether they take pride in their work. It is usually fairly obvious whether they consider doing a good job a priority. A quick glance at most people will show you what value a healthy diet and good exercise has in their life. Or you can drive by someone's home and see whether they consider keeping their landscaping nice important. You can then walk into their home and conclude quickly if they regard cleanliness in their personal spaces as a major concern. Simple observation can indicate what a person's priorities are all about for a lot of things.

But one thing nobody in a church can determine by just looking at another individual is whether God's work is a financial priority or not. You can glance at how a person dresses and come to all kinds of conclusions, but one that you cannot draw is how much they have given to God's work. That's because in the Seventh-day Adventist Church most giving takes place in a way that doesn't bring attention to the giver.

When the offering plate gets passed around, we don't stand up with trumpets blasting to announce that we are going to donate an extra $20 for the children's offering on that particular day.

When Jesus talks about money, He makes it a matter of priority because He knows that giving isn't some rote exercise that doesn't mean anything. He recognizes that it is a matter of the heart.

Unless you could sit down with a person and look at their checkbook ledger, you wouldn't be able to give an honest opinion about how people donate to God's work. That being said, your checkbook does do a good job of reflecting where your priorities are.

Once, for a bit of self-examination, I took a look at what the priorities of my local congregation were:

1. Tithe. About 60 percent of the attendees in my local church gave God 10 percent of their income as tithe.

2. I would say that another priority reflected through giving was to make sure our children grew up with every chance to develop a relationship with Jesus. The most money we spent in that church had to do with our school, our youth, and our Pathfinder programs. That says something, doesn't it?

3. That congregation paid off a land debt of $1.2 million in seven years. They had a serious commitment to getting out of debt.

4. About 40 percent of people who attended my church offered something to sustain its operations and ministries, help with outreach and evangelism, and pay for Sabbath school periodicals and janitorial services.

Yet as I considered its mission statement I had to wonder: Does our budget accurately reflect what we say we are all about?

If you were to examine a church's budget, I think you would be able to get a pretty clear idea of where their priorities lie as a church. Some people might say those priorities are good, while others would suggest that they could be rearranged to reflect more of this and less of that.

But what about you? If Jesus were to sit down next to you with a spreadsheet of how you spend your money each month, what would He say were your big priorities according to how you manage your finances?

Earlier in this book I suggested that when a family received each paycheck they should set it on a table, gather around it, and thank God for the money He'd provided them with. I wonder how they would spend that money if it were dedicated to the Lord.

If it is true that how you use your money to bless God's mission on earth reflects your priorities—your very dedication to His mission—what would a glance at your bank statement say about your feelings toward His work through your local church?

Now, I want to get something straight here: when Jesus says, "Do not store up for yourselves treasures on earth, where moths and vermin destroy, and where thieves break in and steal. But store up for yourselves treasures in heaven, where moths and vermin do not destroy, and where thieves do not break in and steal," I don't think He is asking us to take our paychecks and sign them over to the church. I'm pretty sure He isn't asking us to live in a cardboard box just so that the church can thrive.

Rather, I think that if you want to know what the crux of Jesus' point is here, you have to go to the next sentence: "For where your treasure is, there your heart will be also."

Where is your treasure?

In Luke 10 Jesus speaks to a friend about where her treasure was. "As Jesus and his disciples were on their way, he came to a village where a woman named Martha opened her home to him. She had a sister called Mary, who sat at the Lord's feet listening to what he said. But Martha was distracted by all the preparations that had to be made. She came to him and asked, 'Lord, don't you care that my sister has left me to do the work by myself? Tell her to help me!' 'Martha, Martha,' the Lord answered, 'you are worried and upset about many things, but few things are needed—or indeed only one. Mary has chosen what is better, and it will not be taken away from her' " (Luke 10:38-42).

Mary's heart was at the feet of Jesus. And it showed. If you were to look at her checkbook ledger (if she would have had one), you would have seen that priority reflected there. How she lived reflected her treasure and her heart.

In the book *Steps to Christ* Ellen White asks a simple question and gives a simple answer. Her question? "By what means, then, shall we determine whose side we are on?"

The next paragraph doesn't look at the outward appearance, but at the heart. Here's her answer: "Who has the heart? With whom are our thoughts? Of whom do we love to converse? Who has our warmest affections and our best energies?" (p. 58).

I would submit to you that we will find the answer to such questions indicated by how we give of both ourselves and how of our funds.

Jesus, in the Sermon on the Mount, speaks of our priorities. One way to tell where our priorities as a church and as individuals are is by a quick look at where we invest our treasure.

You might say, "Well, Pastor, I don't have enough treasure to measure!"

If this is how you feel, I have a story for you.

"As Jesus looked up, he saw the rich putting their gifts into the temple treasury. He also saw a poor widow put in two very small copper coins. 'Truly I tell you,' he said, 'this poor widow has put in more than all the others. All these people gave their gifts out of their wealth; but she out of her poverty put in all she had to live on' " (Luke 21:1-4).

With Jesus the amount of money one invests in the kingdom isn't what's important. Rather, the intent, the heart behind the gift, is what's vital.

What's your priority?

I have a relative that had the gift of making money. It seemed that if he slipped and fell, he'd fall into a pile of money. And he loved to make money too. He was good at it.

I happen to believe that it was a spiritual gift! He was a millionaire many times over. And the more he made, the harder his heart became. His marriages dissolved, his kids fought over material things, his family was not a happy one.

When he died, he died with lots of stuff.

I don't want to die with lots of stuff. What am I going to do with it after I die?

In the movie *Remember the Titans* the new coach of the high school football team attempts to make a point to two rebellious team members that have made it known that they don't want to play for a Black coach.

Before he lets them on the bus they have to answer a question that he asks them. He comes up real close and says, "Who's your daddy?" And he won't let them on the bus until they say, "You're my daddy."

In other words, to whom are you going to submit? To whom are you going to turn your will over to? Jesus makes the same point in Matthew 6:24 when He says, "No one can serve two masters. Either you will hate the one and love the other, or you will be devoted to the one and despise the other. You cannot serve both God and money."

Here's my question: Are you the master of your finances, or are your finances the master of you?

I hate being a slave.

When I was a teenager, I thought it would look cool if I started smoking. I continued for about two years until one day I realized that I wasn't choosing cigarettes, they were choosing me. I was riding down the highway with a cigarette in my mouth one summer day with my window partway down. The wind swirled the smoke and ashes around my head and into my eyes. As I winced and tried to avoid ash in my eyes, I suddenly realized how ridiculous it was for me to be a slave of something that I needed so badly that I would sacrifice my own safety and comfort to have it. Wadding up the cigarette package, I threw it out my window with the lit cigarette and haven't smoked since. Because I hated being a slave to it, I became its master.

Isn't it tragic when we see our loved ones give their lives over to be slaves to drugs or alcohol? I would submit to you that it's just as tragic when we become slaves to our money.

Jesus, in the Sermon on the Mount, challenges us to become the master of our money. He says that we can't serve both God and it. If we are living month to month serving our money, it means that we don't have the choice to give what we want, because we are too busy trying to catch up with past due bills and credit card payments. We've gotten ourselves into a situation in which our habits dictate how we spend our money.

Jesus says that when money becomes our master, it's not a good thing.

Some people in my life constantly complain about not having enough money. They are always late on their bills and don't have the kind of credit score that would buy them a candy bar. Nor do they give anything to the church and its work.

But guess where they spend at least one Saturday night per month? At the casino. Money is their master.

Nothing can squelch the salvation right out of us more than having money be our master.

When Jesus told the parable of the sower, He said that the thorns that choked the life out of what could have been good seed were the worries of this life and the love of money and things.

So why would Jesus spend time talking about our priorities with money? Is it because He wanted to take up an offering after He finished preaching that day? Was it because He wanted to become rich by taking all the people's money before they left the side of the mountain?

No. Jesus knows that we are going to be happier and more satisfied people when we give. Nothing feels better than when we contribute with a cheerful heart. Whether we share of our time, our efforts, or our money, the Lord knows that we then become more like God and adopt His character.

God is love. And out of love He has supplied us with all our needs. He didn't just kind of give of Himself to save us. Nor did He just kind of forgive us. He went all out when He sent His Son. When we learn to be "all out" with the most personal part of ourselves—our finances—we actually become more and more like our Father in heaven who is all out for us.

So how about it? Why not put forth an effort to get our priorities straight? Why not take a moment of time when we get our paycheck, bow our head over it, and thank God for the money we've received that month? And then why not dedicate every penny we spend to His glory?

CHAPTER **21**

Jesus, The Passover Lamb

Suppose that I gave you an envelope that came from God informing you that this Sunday at 2:00 p.m., as you tried to cross Highway 20, a 2015 GMC truck would smash into you and you would die at the scene?

What would you be doing this Sunday at 2:00 p.m.?

Maybe you'd somehow find your way downtown to a hotel on Saturday night, and on Sunday you'd remain in the room. You might stay as far away from Highway 20 as you possibly could that day.

But what if the divine note that announced your death included an addendum that said, "And if you don't run away from death, your children will have the best life they could ever have. They will have deep faith and joy that they couldn't have without your death. Oh, and at the resurrection, you will have eternal life."

Now what would you do? Would you be willing to die for eternal security and your children's happiness?

Jesus faced just that proposition. The letter He read was the law and the prophets. And as Jesus realized that the law and the prophets all pointed to Him, He actually realized and understood when and how He was going to be killed—not in a random car accident, but by the very people He came to enlighten and redeem. He told His disciples, "As you know, the Passover is two days away—and the Son of Man will be handed over to be crucified" (Matt. 26:2).

Jesus, two days before His death, was already aware of what was going to happen to Him, and yet instead of hightailing it away from Jerusalem, He took the disciples to the very place where He knew He would meet His demise.

So how did Jesus know when He was going to die? It seems as if He were aware of it for a while. On occasion He would tell people, "It's not the time or the hour for Me." But now He doesn't fight His impending fate. What convinced Him that His time had now come?

I would like to suggest that Jesus recognized when His death approached because He was a student of Scripture. First, He knew the year of His death, because He was familiar with the book of Daniel.

The 490-day prophecy of Daniel 9 predicts the Messiah being cut off or killed in the middle of the prophetic week. Jesus knew that that very year His own rebellious children would have Him put to death.

That remarkable prophecy narrowed it down to the year, but how could He have determined the very day and hour of His crucifixion?

We find the first clue in the book of Exodus: "For seven days you are to eat bread made without yeast. On the first day remove the yeast from your houses, for whoever eats anything with yeast in it from the first day through the seventh must be cut off from Israel. On the first day hold a sacred assembly, and another one on the seventh day. Do no work at all on these days, except to prepare food for everyone to eat; that is all you may do. Celebrate the Feast of Unleavened Bread, because it was on this very day that I brought your divisions out of Egypt. Celebrate this day as a lasting ordinance for the generations to come. In the first month you are to eat bread made without yeast, from the evening of the fourteenth day until the evening of the twenty-first day" (Ex. 12:15-18).

The first month of the Jewish calendar is called Nissan. For Jesus' whole life every fourteenth day of Nissan He and His family celebrated Passover. Jews slew the lamb in remembrance of how God delivered His people out of bondage and into freedom.

And Jesus realized that He was the Passover Lamb. John yelled it from the Jordan, "Behold, the Lamb of God who takes away the sin of the world!" (John 1:29, NASB).

Paul shared Jesus' understanding. "Get rid of the old yeast, so that you may be a new unleavened batch—as you really are. For Christ, our Passover lamb, has been sacrificed" (1 Cor. 5:7).

Jesus knew that His life would end when the priests slaughtered the Passover lamb during that very year. And He knew how it was going to happen because He realized that the Old Testament was speaking of Him.

He recognized that David was speaking of Him when he wrote, "My God, my God, why have you forsaken me? Why are you so far from saving me, so far from my cries of anguish? . . . All who see me mock me; they hurl insults, shaking their heads. 'He trusts in the Lord,' they say, 'let the Lord rescue him. Let him deliver him, since he delights in him.' . . . I am poured out like water, and all my bones are out of joint. My heart has turned to wax; it has melted away within me. My mouth is dried up like a potsherd, and my tongue sticks to the roof of my mouth; you lay me in the dust of death. Dogs surround me, a pack of villains encircles me; they pierce my hands and my feet. All my bones are on display; people stare and gloat over me. They divide my clothes among them and cast lots for my garment" (Ps. 22:1-18).

Jesus knew Isaiah was speaking of Him: "But he was pierced for our transgressions, he was crushed for our iniquities; the punishment that brought us peace was on him, and by his wounds we are healed. We all, like sheep, have gone astray, each of us has turned to his own way; and the Lord has laid on him the iniquity of us all. He was oppressed and afflicted, yet he did not open his mouth; he was led like a lamb to the slaughter, and as a sheep before its shearers is silent, so he did not open his mouth" (Isa. 53:5-7).

The day before He was to die, Jesus sat down with His disciples to prepare them for this terrible truth. In John 13 through 17 Jesus essentially speaks His last words to them. The Bible seems to indicate that He ate that last Passover supper with His disciples a day early as suggested by John 18:28: "Then the Jewish leaders took Jesus from Caiaphas to the palace of the Roman governor. By now it was early morning, and to avoid ceremonial uncleanness they did not enter the palace, because they wanted to be able to eat the Passover." The Passover had not yet taken place. I think He celebrated beforehand because He wanted to have time with His friends, to give them His last message before He died.

Jesus knows the year, the day, and the very hour of His death, and what does He do? Does He run for His life? Does He quickly ascend to heaven so that He can escape the suffering? No. The consequences are too dire. He's thinking not of Himself but of His children. He teaches them one more time the lesson of humility when He washes their feet.

And then, knowing that there would no longer be any need to sacrifice a lamb, the Lamb of God holds up the bread and tells the disciples, "Take, eat, this is My body." Picking up the cup, He says, "Take, drink, this is My blood."

Finally, Jesus goes to the cross the very day that the Passover Lamb is to be slain.

And as Jesus hung on the cross, Jesus uttered the words "Father, unto Thy hands I commit My Spirit," and He died just as the Passover lamb was being slaughtered in the city; just as the Bible had foretold so many years before.

Today we celebrate the new Passover. Known as the Lord's Supper, its bread and the wine are symbols of our faith in Jesus' sacrifice. When we eat the bread and drink the juice, we realize that it was our sin that crushed the life out of Jesus, and because of that, death passes over us and we receive eternal life.

The Communion service is a vital part of the Christian faith, because Jesus set it up that way. He knew that in the old sacrificial system a sacrifice was not finished until the person who brought it ate a piece of the offering.

When that lamb became a part of their body, then the sacrifice was complete.

Jesus said to His disciples, “Unless you eat My flesh and drink My blood, you can have no part of Me.” This, of course, freaked most of His followers out. They left shaking their heads.

Today we know that Jesus was speaking of the symbols of the Last Supper, the bread and the wine. When we take those symbols we symbolically make the Lamb of God a part of our body, just like a Hebrew in the Old Testament ate the Passover lamb to incorporate it into their body. This eating of the Lamb (symbolically) is our declaration that Christ lives in us and through us. It’s a beautiful symbol of how Christ in us is our hope of glory.

CHAPTER **22**

Imagine for a moment the worst thing that a parent could ever go through. Your child is sick, and you can see that the illness is more severe than just a cold or flu. When you take him or her to the doctor for an examination; at first there doesn't seem to be a reason for big concern, but then, when the blood test comes back, the doctor shares the bad news—she suspects it's cancer.

Further testing confirms the doctor's initial suspicions. Your child has cancer, and even with radical treatment the physicians all agree that in only a matter of months, maybe weeks, your son or daughter will die.

You love your child more than you do your own life, and you would gladly change places with them. With utmost grief you realize that you will never get to see them be baptized, get their driver's license, graduate, or wed. The prognosis is grim, and the outcome is sure. Your beloved, the one you would gladly die for, is going to suffer and die right before your very eyes.

Now imagine with me one more thing: *You have the power to heal your child by just speaking the word that it be so.* But you don't. For reasons that completely bewilder all your friends and family, you don't speak healing into your child. Instead, you watch and comfort your child as they slowly suffer toward death.

The pain you feel as their parent is excruciating. You hate seeing them suffer. It brings you to tears every time they cry out in pain. Yet you don't do what you are capable of doing—you don't heal them.

The people around you start to scoff. They begin to think that maybe you aren't such a good parent. Perhaps there is a sadistic dark side to you that nobody knew about. As a result they begin to call you names—names that you know in your heart you don't deserve. But although you love your child with an everlasting love and want to speak that healing word, you don't. For some reason, you choose to comfort them through their pain until they are finally laid to rest.

That is the paradox of the Lamb as described in Revelation 5.

Revelation 5:6 describes Jesus in symbolic terms as a lamb that looks as if it has been slain or slaughtered, but is alive now. And this strange-appearing Lamb that is on the throne of the universe has seven eyes and seven horns.

I suppose I should state the obvious here: the Lamb that appears as if it has been slaughtered yet lives is . . . not a hard symbol to figure out, is it? Jesus. He is the Lamb of God.

As you probably know, the number seven is an ancient biblical symbol of perfection. So to take a little liberty with the text, Jesus has perfect eyes and perfect horns.

Another common symbol in prophecy is the horn. In prophecy horns usually stand for power. So Jesus, who sits on the throne, has perfect eyes and perfect power.

And what do we make of the eyes on this strange-looking creature? Does "perfect eyes" mean that Jesus has 20/20 vision? Well, kind of.

The perfect eyes of the Lamb represent the reality that Jesus sees and experiences everything that goes on in the universe as though He were standing right where it happened. He isn't just aware of it—He sees it as though He's experiencing it firsthand. This isn't the story of a parent who is overseas and hears of their child's death. That would be bad enough. No, Jesus' perfect eyes tell us that He is the parent that has to witness the death of His child as though He were standing there and watching it take place.

The Lamb of Revelation 5 is the symbol of Jesus who has all power (He has the ability to do whatever He wants) and all experiential vision (He sees, realizes, and feels all).

If it's true that Jesus loves us even more than He loves Himself, can you imagine what He must endure moment by moment as He watches His beloved suffer and die from day to day on our sin-sick earth?

And yet He seemingly does nothing about it. OK, I know that sometimes miracles happen and cancer disappears and people get healed. I have witnessed my share of the miraculous. But the number of times I've seen the miraculous versus the number of times I've stood graveside with grieving loved ones doesn't even compare.

If the Lamb views all that we are going through and has perfect power to make it all go away, why doesn't He?

Well, this is not an easy subject, and certainly there is no easy answer to such a question. Nothing I write in this book is going to make a mother who has lost her child gasp with a grand theological aha moment that will make all things well.

Yet I think it's important that we try to understand the big picture that the Lamb (the one delivering this message to John) is trying to convey about the character of God and the destiny of His people.

It's critical to remember that the book of Revelation depicts more than one lamb. There is the Lamb who sits on the throne and has seven horns and seven eyes. But there is also a lamb in Revelation 13.

The beast that produces this lamb in Revelation 13 has also received a fatal wound that it had been healed of, just like the Lamb on the throne. And this beast/lamb has authority too. It wields its power and tells people what to do.

The lamb in Revelation 13 puts a mark or a seal on his followers. So does the Lamb in Revelation 5.

The lamb in Revelation 13 receives worship. So does the Lamb in Revelation 5.

The lamb in Revelation 13 is a part of a system that had a prophetic three and a half years (spoken of seven times in Daniel and Revelation as 42 months, 1260 days, and time, times, and a half a time) to do its best to show the universe its interpretation of who God is. The Lamb in Revelation 5 came to earth and for three and a half years and showed the world the true character of the Father.

For sure, we find a lot of similarities in prophecy between the two lambs. But the biggest difference between the Revelation 5 Lamb and the Revelation 13 lamb is that the Revelation 13 lamb only looks like a lamb, but speaks like a dragon (see Rev. 13:11).

One Lamb is the pure and true representation of the Father. The other lamb is a pretender in league with the dragon of Revelation to distort and warp God's character. He is out to do damage and make a counterfeit of every good and perfect gift that the Lamb of Revelation 5 has given to humanity on earth.

And the counterfeit lamb isn't trying to mislead the already-deluded. He seeks to deceive even the very elect, if that were possible.

So what's the deal with the false lamb—the one who resembles a lamb but roars like a dragon? And what does this have to do with the Lamb of Revelation 5 having to sit and watch His children suffer?

The Lamb of Revelation 5, when He came to earth as a man, revealed to us that God the Father is love. *Love* is the one word that best describes the Father. And the opposite of love is not hate, but control. And love, by nature, cannot do that.

The biggest difference between the false lamb and the Lamb of God is that the false lamb demands worship. It forces and coerces praise and adulation. The beast that looks like a lamb but speaks like a dragon does not honor free choice. It threatens economic sanctions and even death if you don't worship it.

The Lamb of God invites, woos, and extends grace. Always patiently waiting for a response, He says, "Come unto Me, and I will give you rest." No control. Just love.

You see, love is the opposite of control.

Imagine a husband who dictated every move and every decision his wife made. He controlled what she ate, where she spent her time, how much money she could have, the route she would drive to the store, the clothing she wore each day . . . Would you call him a loving spouse?

This is not love. By its very nature, love cannot control. Love is synonymous with freedom. And God is love.

As we look at the great controversy we see a conflict raging between God and Satan. Satan had to leave heaven because of it and landed here on earth. Our world is the battleground over the character of God.

Satan seized the first victory in the Garden of Eden. He staked his claim over humanity as soon as he was able to get Adam and Eve to question God's character. At that point he became the prince of the world, the ruler of the air. Humanity has felt his sting ever since.

I can imagine that God wanted to swoop in at the last minute and rescue Adam and Eve from the choice they were about to make, but He couldn't. Love doesn't force. It presents its best case and then grants thinking individuals the freedom to choose.

And here we are in the twenty-first century still feeling the curse of sin. Why doesn't God just swoop down and heal all the Christian kids with cancer? Why doesn't He intervene on our behalf when we need Him to? After all, He has perfect power and has perfect vision of the situation. Why can't He rescue me, or you, or my kid?

Two suggestions:

1. If He can, He does. But usually He doesn't get involved unless asked. When asked *and* if He can, He always does. I believe that prayer is the act of giving God permission to involve Himself in our lives.

2. When He can't, it's not because He doesn't long to, but rather because He can't. Not that He isn't all-powerful. But for God to swoop in and rescue every believer from every peril that befalls them would give Satan the ability to say, "See, You treat them just like Job. They serve You only because of what You give them."

So, for now, we live in this world. Satan stole the ownership papers for the earth at that tree in the garden. Jesus took back those documents on another tree—Golgotha. And now we live between the kingdom of God on this earth and the kingdom to come.

The Bible explains it this way: "The race is not to the swift and the battle is not to the warriors, and neither is bread to the wise nor wealth to the discerning nor favor to men of ability; *for time and chance overtake them all*" (Eccl. 9:11, NASB).

It's not that I'm a deist. I do believe that God gets involved in human affairs. But He is not a dictator, a control freak. He has stepped back and allowed human beings even greater freedom. If He had kept direct control, I believe this world would be very different than it is now. Because He allows so much freedom, elements of time and chance overtake us all, just as the Bible says.

"The heavens are the heavens of the Lord, but the earth He has given to the sons of men" (Ps. 115:16, NASB).

In a sense, we asked for it. We (the human race) ripped control of our lives out of the hand of God at the garden because we mistook Him for something He is not. And we've been viewing Him as something other than a God of love ever since.

Can you imagine the pain Jesus must feel as He has to watch the whole controversy play itself out? Although His children are crying out for deliverance, He has permitted His hands to be bound. He can intervene only in limited ways. Most of His children have such a warped view of who He is that they actually attribute evil to Him and His character. They call natural disasters "acts of God." Even worse, they brutalize one another in His name, because they think that's what He would want and that's what He is like. Every time we attribute something evil and hurtful to God's doing, we put another spike in His hands and feet.

The Lamb who has perfect eyes wants to rescue us from the world. He longs to break into human history and erase all the pain. And in a sense He did.

The Lamb—the Lamb on the throne—came to clarify the Father. And we disagreed with Him so vehemently that we killed Him.

The whole book of Revelation is about how the once-dead-but-now-resurrected Lamb goes to battle with the beast over who God is. And in the end? The Lamb of God wins out over the beast that looks like a lamb and sounds like a dragon. The love of the Lamb wins out over the rage of the dragon. The Lamb woos His followers and gives them His mark on their foreheads. The beast enslaves his followers and brands them with his mark on their forehead and on their right hands.

When this final event in earth's history takes place, that's when things change. That's when God's character gets vindicated. That's when God will be able to soothe all our aches and throw sin and death into that lake of fire. And that's when tears will be wiped away and love will win the day.

So between now and then, I would highly suggest: Follow the Lamb. He knows just where to lead you. Through every trial and every disaster that may fall upon you, He knows how to get you over that finish line. Follow the Lamb wherever He leads you, and you will one day understand.

Never let go of the Lamb.

Notes:

Notes:

Notes:

Notes:

Me, Preach an Evangelistic Series? Why Not!

Created by David Asscherick and Ty Gibson

All around the world, people your age are preaching for evangelistic meetings. Why not you?

We make it easy with a series of sermons written by David Asscherick and Ty Gibson. *The One* includes 12 Christ-centered presentations that can be quickly learned and easily personalized. *The One* can help anyone experience the excitement of preaching the gospel . . . even you.

Prices and availability subject to change. Canadian prices higher.

Scan this to learn more.

AdventistBookCenter.com | 800.765.6955

Review&Herald®
Spread the Word